STRATEGIC CHOICES, ETHICAL DILEMMAS

'An exciting and unique contribution to addressing modern economic and political problems via a wonderful, ancient epic'—Jagdish Bhagwati, economist, and university professor of economics and law, Columbia University

'This is a book that was waiting to be written, perhaps the first of several such. The Mahabharat is of perennial interest because individual ethical dilemmas and conflicts of dharma resonate thousands of years later. However, unlike something like the *Arthashastr*, the Mahabharat's rich tapestry has been relatively unexplored for collective public policy choices and strategic decisions, even in cross-country negotiations. With their rich academic and research experience and deep understanding of this "Itihasa", Aruna Narlikar, Amitabh Mattoo and Amrita Narlikar have produced a wonderful exploration, using specific incidents to push the envelope of Mahabharat research further'—Bibek Debroy, economist, and chairman of the Economic Advisory Council to the Prime Minister of India

'A remarkable book that shows how the rich content of ancient texts produced by centuries of ancient Indian statecraft can and should be used to inform our present debates on issues of foreign and security policy and their ethics. Avoiding the mistake of claiming that all solutions for present issues are to be found in these texts, it uses the Mahabharat to conceptualize and to prompt fresh thinking. If there is a beginning to an Indian school of international relations, it is in a work like this, grounded in our past but not trapped by it. That there are similarities between the world of the Mahabharat and today's international situation makes it even more relevant. A book that the scholar, practitioner, interested layperson and all of us who have been brought up in the conceptual universe of the Mahabharat must read'—Shivshankar Menon, former foreign secretary and former national security adviser of India

'All the classics of world literature capture the enduring ethical dilemmas of life but none does more expansively than the Mahabharat. In this elegant and enchanting volume, Aruna Narlikar, Amitabh Mattoo and Amrita Narlikar retell the ancient stories from the Mahabharat to help us reflect and cope with the multiple moral dilemmas of modern life'—C. Raja Mohan, writer and columnist

'The ancient Indian epic the Mahabharat is a timeless marvel that highlights and teaches human fragilities, competitions and challenges, even while pursuing larger goals through nobler paths. Using this timeless wonder, *Strategic Choices, Ethical Dilemmas* seeks to address the perennial confrontation between realpolitik and ethics. I wish to congratulate the three illustrious scholars on their efforts to seek answers to modern foreign policy challenges facing India through the prism of the ancient wisdom exhibited in the Mahabharat. Indeed, bringing in the Bharatiya narratives will be a valuable addition'—Santishree Pandit, vice chancellor, Jawaharlal Nehru University

'This is a book that could not be timelier. Coming as it does amidst rapidly changing global realities, this unique perspective from Dr Aruna Narlikar, Prof. Amitabh Mattoo and Prof. Amrita Narlikar is a refreshing departure from conventional approaches to strategic theory.

'Drawing from the timeless wisdom of the Mahabharat, this masterful presentation culls out the lessons ensconced in the epic's colourful legends, which are salient to today's strategic and political dilemmas.

'The earnestness with which the authors seek to demonstrate that it is "possible to win and still keep one's soul" and that "humanity" in its most inclusive sense can still be recovered, is indeed a refreshing tonic in these jaded times.

'I strongly recommend this book to readers seeking fresh narrations of the Indian story. The reader is bound to find enchanting the lessons in the timeless stories as they are retold here, in this book, and to come away inspired by the noble morality of Yudhishthir, whose emphasis on dharma makes clear there doesn't have to be a dichotomy between interests and values'—Malini Parthasarathy, former editor, *The Hindu*, and former chairperson, The Hindu Group

'The author trio have set out to share with their readers the universal lessons that the ancient story of the Mahabharat offers. Treating the Mahabharat as a manual for modern day, the episodes quoted illustrate clearly how the Mahabharat's message is seen as relevant for today. The authors explain this in simple, beautifully crafted words'—Nirmala Sitharaman, finance minister of India

'*Strategic Choices, Ethical Dilemmas: Stories from the Mahabharat* is a brilliant disquisition on the timeless lessons in statecraft, foreign policy and societal organization that can be derived from the Mahabharat. Engaging and insightful, the authorial trio's seasoned expertise is on excellent display as they unpack why the epic is relevant to global politics centuries after it was first told. Epochs change, human nature rarely does! A thoroughly enjoyable, diverting and instructive read'—Shashi Tharoor, former minister and Member of the Lok Sabha

STRATEGIC CHOICES, ETHICAL DILEMMAS

STORIES FROM THE MAHABHARAT

ARUNA NARLIKAR
AMITABH MATTOO
AMRITA NARLIKAR

VINTAGE
An imprint of Penguin Random House

VINTAGE

USA | Canada | UK | Ireland | Australia
New Zealand | India | South Africa | China | Singapore

Vintage is part of the Penguin Random House group of companies
whose addresses can be found at global.penguinrandomhouse.com

Published by Penguin Random House India Pvt. Ltd
4th Floor, Capital Tower 1, MG Road,
Gurugram 122 002, Haryana, India

Penguin
Random House
India

First published in Vintage by Penguin Random House India 2023

10 9 8 7 6 5 4 3 2

The views and opinions expressed in this book are the authors' own and the facts are as
reported by them which have been verified to the extent possible, and the publishers are
not in any way liable for the same.

ISBN 9780143459750

Typeset in Sabon by Manipal Technologies Limited, Manipal

Printed at Repro India Limited

www.penguin.co.in

MIX
Paper from
responsible sources
FSC® C047271

This is a legitimate digitally printed version of the book and therefore might not
have certain extra finishing on the cover.

To

The Divine Scribe
Vighneshwar-Vighnaharta

Mahadevi Ambabai
of Kolhapur

Maej Kheer Bhavani and Maej Sharika Devi
of Kashmir

In humble devotion,
And with boundless gratitude

Contents

1

Introduction

The Mahabharat as a Manual for the Modern Day

Our current existence is blessed with a remarkable set of opportunities, but scratch below the surface and it is impossible to escape the dilemmas and trade-offs that this often selective and skewed overabundance entails.

Some of the choices we make as individuals may appear to be inconsequential. But these individual choices can have collective consequences, and sometimes, even the smallest action by one seemingly insignificant individual can make a huge difference. Indeed, in a world of intense interconnectedness and high uncertainty, it may not be far-fetched to see a social version of the butterfly effect at work.[1] An extreme and negative example of this is the case of the Italian marathon runner who is believed to have acted as super-spreader of Covid-19 in the early days of the pandemic.[2]

Occasionally, the options we are presented with seem straightforward enough. For instance, if asked, we would almost certainly refuse to buy products made from ivory to support the efficacy of ivory bans in order to protect elephants. But many others pose more of a quandary. An ethically minded consumer might legitimately wonder: do I buy glass bangles that were probably produced by child labour and contribute to an exploitative industry, or do

I boycott these and consign the poor producers of these products to even greater penury? Do I really have the right to deprive animals of their lives for meat and other products (often farmed or procured under conditions of great cruelty), even though organically and ethically sourced vegan foods are too expensive for my daily wage?

Further, the choices themselves are not restricted to the level of the individual; policy choices made by governments can have life and death consequences for large groups of people. Examples include lockdowns and restrictions to save lives versus removal of restrictions to save the economy; investment in cheaper coal to achieve quick and much-needed growth versus investment in more expensive green technology to achieve sustainable, climate-friendly growth; deepening relations with authoritarian states (to ensure continued profit for investors) or decoupling (to secure supply chains at the cost of short-term profits).

Think too much on these dilemmas and one risks getting paralysed into inaction. But inaction is not and cannot be the answer. Climate change is wreaking havoc across countries and local communities. Human misdeeds—past and present—continue to cause horrific suffering amongst animals, and wildlife populations have declined by almost 70 per cent in the last forty-nine years.[3] Not inaction, but *correct* action is needed: a mindful awareness of the consequences of our actions, and then an ability to create and make wise choices.

We are patently aware of the gravity of the real-world threats and predicaments that face the planet and all its residents. But sometimes, the answers are looking us in the eye, and yet, we still fail to see them amidst daily distractions and difficulties. Some of these answers lie deep within our own selves and our culture—in the powerful and still largely untapped traditions and wisdom of our ancient texts. And in dire times like these, there is perhaps no text better suited to inspire and guide than the Mahabharat.

Why the Mahabharat, and why our book?

India, with its wide-ranging pantheon of religions and philosophies, is a good place to start when searching for spiritual texts that offer time-tested answers to tough questions. Admittedly, not all ancient wisdom contains full-blown and tailor-made answers to current problems. But sometimes, it is useful to return to the kernels of truth that our ancient texts can offer, rather than reinvent wheels and make them square. And in the treasure trove of spiritual texts to be found in India, the epics—the Mahabharat and the Ramayan—occupy a special place. The richness of their stories has long carried not only intellectual heft but also popular appeal. They make for multi-layered readings, narrations, interpretations and analyses. And while both epics are deeply embedded in our collective imagination, the differences between them also stand out.

The Ramayan is, at its core, a text about ideals. Lord Ram, for instance, is the ideal hero in every moral and martial sense; he, his faithful wife (Sita), loyal brother (Lakshman) and trusted ally (Hanuman) teach us of all the virtues that should inspire us. The Mahabharat is more complex—not just for its extraordinary length of 1,00,000 verses. Accrued over the centuries, these verses have been shaped and reshaped through oral traditions and retellings. The heroes of this epic are many, but they are far from perfect. The always truthful and gentle

Yudhishthir knowingly speaks a lie that produces its intended, devastating effect on his guru, Dronaacharya. The brave Arjun shoots his arrows, using a woman as a shield, fatally wounding the beloved, and otherwise undefeatable grandsire, Bhishm. Even Lord Krishn— who is revealed to be not just a god but God—shows himself willing to resort to guile and deceit. And just as its heroes show human frailties and flaws, many villains of the Mahabharat show some unexpected virtues. Karn is ferociously loyal and generous to a fault. Even Duryodhan, whose unbridled ambition and unreasonable demands—such as the pronouncement that he will not cede even five villages to his Pandav cousins—provide a major cause for the great war within the Bharat dynasty, shows exceptional courage and a sense of fair play in many of his dealings. Both men and women, on both sides of the warring parties, reveal themselves to be capable of extreme cruelty and also display acts of unparalleled valour and kindness. Unlike the protagonists of the Ramayan, the characters of the Mahabharat are as complex, multifaceted and torn as we are today.[4]

The world of the Mahabharat is often polarized and brutal, and in this sense too, the epic offers some parallels with the challenging times we live in now. The text is commonly assumed to be a story primarily of war, as indicated by the fact that the word 'Mahabharat' is used synonymously with war in modern-day Hindi. The great epic is certainly a terrific source for understanding concepts of war strategy in ancient India. But it is much more than 'just' a treatise on war. In fact, only five of its eighteen parts (parvs) are about the eighteen-day war. The rest of the epic, and even the parts that deal directly with the war, are infused with profound normative questions of (and advice on) morality, duty, virtue and law. It provides us with tragic examples of how not to treat the environment (epitomized in the burning of the Khandav forest), but it also offers us heart-warming illustrations of the moral and material benefits—and many ways—of living in harmony with nature. It even includes within it the Bhagavad Gita—the Divine Song—which many regard as the heart of Hindu philosophy. The text also does not shy away from pragmatic and strategic issues of negotiation, alliances, training and education, leadership and more.

Its unflinching look at bleak realities makes the Mahabharat a text uniquely applicable to our current times. In its pages are lessons on how to overcome the harshness and misery of life, and how to do so without resorting to a relativism of values or an advocacy of other-worldliness. Its chapters are replete with guidance on how to thrive in the battlefields of life and dharm, and how to be a *karmyogi* (one who attains personal fulfilment and spiritual salvation through his work, while living the worldly life). Our purpose is to draw on these lessons to explore winning strategies that work hand in hand with ethical choices.

The structure of the book

This introductory chapter is followed by a 'cheat-sheet' that summarizes the plot line and structure of the Mahabharat. We recognize that summarizing an ancient epic of 1,00,000 Sanskrit verses is no small task. But we believe this is important, both as a reminder for our readers in India and for an engaged, international audience that may be less conversant with the complex plot line of the Mahabharat. And then, we dive into the remarkable ocean of stories, sharing with our readers some of our old-time and newly discovered favourites.

Chapters 3 to 11 contain a story each, with each of these chapters comprising three parts. The first part is devoted to narrating an inspiring story from the Mahabharat that has direct relevance to problems of the present. We put our knowledge of Sanskrit and English to work here, such that we might share the original beauty of the poetry of the Mahabharat with the reader, accompanied by our own translations; the narration of the story is conducted with a goal to facilitate access and stoke further interest. The second part applies the insights of the story to the quandaries and dilemmas that people encounter in the precarious business of living their lives. The third section draws out the lessons of the story to political decision-making and focuses especially on questions of foreign policy and international relations.

We have deliberately chosen the medium of stories and brought together a diverse mix of these. This path—as opposed to character studies of the key protagonists or thematic, philosophical interpretations of the epic—has been a surprisingly untrodden one amidst a plethora of interesting writings on the epic. Ultimately though, it is often the stories that people remember and what gets them through tough times. Stories are what bind us with old and new imaginaries. And the Mahabharat has some cracking good stories, some of which we wanted to share with the world.

We also decided to go with an unusual mix of stories. Some, which we draw on, are long-loved favourites of readers within India (savoured via the bedtime stories passed on from grandparents to grandchildren, or in popular culture, e.g. via the televised series of the Mahabharat, directed by B.R. Chopra, which was viewed with dedication across the country in the late 1980s and early 1990s). These stories may also be well-known abroad, not only amongst international scholars with expertise on the Mahabharat but also amongst global citizens maintaining an interest in Indian culture (for instance, via acclaimed British playwright and film-maker Peter Brook's remarkable nine-hour adaptation of the epic for theatre). We think these popular stories are worth investing in, especially as their full meaning and insights are not always reflected upon. But we also did not want our readers to miss out on the loveliness and novelty of some of the more obscure but equally rich stories, and have carefully hand-picked a few of these for our collection as well.[5]

For the purposes of this book, we had a menu of Sanskrit editions of the text to choose from. After careful consideration, we decided against our original inclination to rely solely on the Bhandarkar Oriental Research Institute's (BORI) critical edition of the Mahabharat as our primary source. While this is the most authoritative edition of the epic, and one that we have used extensively for this project too, it is—by its very nature—a trimmed version. We thus also engaged with the longer Ganguly and Gita Press editions because we did not want to lose out on the stories that derive from the powerful oral traditions of the people's Mahabharat that thrive in India even today (but had to be duly weeded out in the BORI project). The story of Ganesh as the scribe for this great epic, for instance, does not find a place in the critical edition; this story, however, is so deeply entrenched in collective memories of the Mahabharat that we could not imagine excluding it from our book.[6]

We also had a variety of spelling formats to choose from. We decided to avoid the anglicized 'Mahabharata', except when an 'a' at the end was necessary to guard against complete mispronunciation (e.g. Dronaacharya, without the 'a' at the end would be grossly misarticulated as 'Dronaacharee'). We resisted the temptation to use diacritical marks: our purpose is to focus on the lessons that the remarkable stories from the epic offer, rather than to bore our reader with pedantic details.

Jugalbandi: authorship and readership

To develop a book like this, founded on the depth of literary knowledge and applying its wide-ranging insights to modern-day life and politics, requires a team of authors. Together, we hope to whet the interest of the Mahabharat novice, offer novel interpretations for the specialist and bring some useful insights from this ancient wisdom to anyone—anywhere—in need of it.

As a team of authors, we combine complementary expertise from literature, security studies, foreign policy analysis, international political economy, negotiation and governance. We draw on our formal expertise in these fields when applying the lessons of the Mahabharat to the present day, and bring our experience in media and management to bear in the advice that the book provides to a wider readership.

We hope that our book will appeal at several levels. There is a burgeoning interest in India's ancient texts today, both within the country of their birth and also internationally. We see this in book publications and articles directly on or making reference to the great epic, as well as in our interactions on social media. As India's power has been rising, outside players are also taking an interest in understanding India on its own terms, rather than through orientalist lenses or Chindia complexes (that tend to conflate the two very different civilizations into a false, 'Asian' homogeneity). To this collection,[7] ours is a unique take that draws on the (well-known and also lesser-known) stories from the Mahabharat and offers their lessons for different aspects of modern life.[8]

Our main motivation is to share with scholars, practitioners and lay readers the invaluable—and universal—lessons that these ancient stories offer for our personal and public lives. Via this book, we aim to bring through some of the pragmatic philosophy, moral strategy and the many other seemingly oxymoronic and still wonderfully timely insights of the Mahabharat. We hope it will assist students in honing their skills of concentration and learning. To practitioners of foreign policy, it will offer new insights on strategy and alliance-building. For policymakers trying to build convincing narratives for climate change mitigation, it will offer new ideas that transcend dominant anthropocentric ones. For the well-intended good citizen, it may throw new light on hidden trade-offs (for instance, between social policy versus green policy). Amidst the extreme discontent that the pandemic and its aftermath continue to generate, it will remind the reader of what we can still cherish and appreciate; that it is possible to win and still keep one's soul; that 'humanity' in its most inclusive sense can still be recovered.

Through its many routes, the Mahabharat contains secrets that can empower all those who seek to put the world to rights. With this book, we share some of the marvellous mysteries of the Mahabharat and hope to bring our readers and ourselves one step closer towards (re-)discovering that elusive notion of dharm together.

2

The Mahabharat: Plot Line and Structure

धर्मे चार्थे च कामे च मोक्षे च भरतर्षभ ।
यदिहास्ति तदन्यत्र, यन्नेहास्ति न तत् क्वचित् ॥

(Dharme chaarthe cha kaame cha Mokshe cha
Bharatarshabh
Yadihaasti tadanyatra, yannehaasti na tat kvachit.)

On the subjects of dharm, material pleasures,
desire and salvation, what is written here may be
found elsewhere,
But what is not in the Mahabharat can be found
nowhere else.

—Mahabharat, I.62.53

The Mahabharat, at its core, is the story of a battle over kingship between two feuding sides of one family. But this is no ordinary battle; it is an existential war between good and evil. At no point are the far-reaching consequences of this war lost on the protagonists,[1] and they are also very present in the minds of readers today. It is perhaps not surprising that in popular parlance, the word 'Mahabharat' is sometimes used synonymously with war.

While there is no doubt that a large chunk of the Mahabharat deals with the ethics, laws and strategy of war,[2] it would be a mistake to regard the epic as solely or even primarily focused on this theme. Its 1,00,000 verses contain within them an impossible richness of wisdom: codes of morality that extend to different spheres of life, manuals of negotiation and treatises on governance. Stories within stories, parables, discourses and sermons give us timeless insights on questions of philosophy and politics. Across its eighteen titanic parts (parvs), we meet some remarkable characters, including heroes whose human frailties teach us vital lessons and villains whose virtues offer moving takeaways. While each one of the human, animal, godly and demonic protagonists is worth getting to know in their own right, in this 'cheat-sheet', we present the heart of the main story: the struggle for power in the Bharat dynasty within the Kuru clan.

King Shantanu, the monarch of Hastinapur, fell in love with Satyavati, the daughter of a chieftain of fishermen, and desired to marry her. The fisherman agreed, but on the condition that Satyavati's progeny would be the heir to the kingdom. Devavrat—born of Shantanu's first marriage to the holy river Ganga—readily renounced his right to the throne. As this did not suffice to persuade Satyavati's father, Devavrat swore to a life of celibacy. With this promise in place, Satyavati and Shantanu would not have to concern themselves with even the possibility of Devavrat fathering children who might compete for the throne. For his willingness to sacrifice his own happiness to ensure that of his father's, Devavrat came to be known as Bhishm—the one who took the terrible vow. For his selflessness, he was blessed with a remarkable boon: no man would be able to kill him in battle, and he would be able to choose the hour of his death.

Bhishm kept his vow and became the 'grandsire' to Satyavati's children: Dhritarashtr and Pandu. Dhritarashtr was blind and Pandu—the younger son—agreed to serve as the regent to the throne. To Dhritarashtr and his wife, Gandhari, were born 100 sons, who came to be known as the Kauravs. The eldest was Duryodhan—courageous, loyal, impulsive and hot-tempered. Pandu had two wives—Kunti and Maadri—but was unable to father children due to a curse. Kunti, however, had been granted a boon: she could call upon any of the gods, if she wished for an offspring. This she did, on Pandu's request, and the five Pandavs were thus born. Three were Kunti's sons: Yudhishthir the just— son of Dharm himself, Bheem the strong—son of Vaayu the wind god, and Arjun the courageous—son of Indr, the king of gods. Kunti also shared her boon with Maadri, to whom were born the handsome twins, Nakul and Sahadev—sons of the Ashwins, physicians to the gods. But there was, in fact, a sixth son, who had been born in secret.

Kunti, when still young and unwed, had been curious to see if the boon that the sage had granted her really worked. She had thus called upon Surya, the sun god, as a test, and found herself mother to a handsome baby boy. Terrified of the shame that would accrue to her as the child had been born out of wedlock, she abandoned her son, who had been born with a distinctive golden armour and golden earrings. A kindly charioteer and his wife, upon finding the child floating in a basket in the river, adopted the boy. This boy turned out to be amongst the truest of the braves of the Mahabharat. He was called Karn—and even today, Indians are proud to name their sons after this hero. But in the Mahabharat, Karn's life was that of a tragic hero. Only Kunti knew the secret of her real first-born; everyone else assumed Yudhishthir to be the eldest Pandav. Karn too believed himself to be of humble birth and endured much ridicule and rejection at the hands of many, including the Pandav brothers and their wife, Draupadi (who had refused to marry the son of a humble charioteer, despite Karn having emerged victorious in a competition to win her hand). In contrast, Duryodhan had treated Karn with respect and offered him his friendship. Loyal to a fault, Karn accepted this offer. At the great battle of Kurukshetra, he would end up fighting courageously—and dying—on the Kaurav side.

From their first encounters, the competition between the Kaurav and Pandav sides was apparent. The cousins learnt the martial arts under the guidance of their grandsire, Bhishm, as well as under the tutelage of the best teachers. These included Dronaacharya and Kripaacharya. Dronaacharya's only and beloved son, Ashwatthama, was schooled together with the princes and showed himself to be as gifted a warrior as the best of the royal pupils. While martial skill was not in short supply in this lively group, there was a difference between the sons of Dhritarashtr and the sons of Pandu: the Pandav brothers showed more temperance than their (usually) more aggressive Kaurav cousins. Even the most quick-tempered amongst the Pandavs and wielder of the mace—Bheem—had kindness, which Duryodhan—comparable both in temper and in proficiency with the same weapon—often lacked.

Gradually, this competition transformed into a ferocious rivalry, which stemmed in good measure from jealousy and resentment on the Kaurav side. Playful combat amongst the boys turned into murderous attempts: from efforts to drown and poison Bheem to a conspiracy to have the entire Pandav family (including their mother) burnt alive in a house of lacquer (Lakshaagraha). Through all these attempts, the Pandav side showed grace, winning the admiration and support of Lord Krishn—a Yaadav king but also an incarnation of Lord Vishnu (the preserver in the Hindu holy trinity).

Dhritarashtr, the blind king, tried to stop the fighting by gifting the Pandavs a part of the kingdom, which they graciously accepted, even though this 'gift' constituted the most uninhabitable and desolate region of Dhritarashtr's domain. Through their bravery, hard work and ability to win hearts and minds, they transformed the bleak terrain into a flourishing kingdom. The capital of the Pandav kingdom was called Indraprasth, and its fame spread far and wide.

Indraprasth—and the success that it symbolized—became the envy of Dhritarashtr's sons. Together with their conniving uncle, Shakuni, Duryodhan and his brothers hatched a plan to cheat the Pandavs of all their achievements, successes and reputation.

Yudhishthir—the most virtuous of the virtuous—had one fatal vice: an addiction to gambling and games of chance. The Pandavs were invited to a game of dice, and Yudhishthir could not refuse the invitation. The dice, in fact, were rigged. Yudhishthir, despite being on an obvious losing streak, staked not only the Pandav kingdom and all their material belongings but also his own person, as well as his brothers and Draupadi. The Kauravs won the game, and the Pandavs lost everything. Duryodhan and his friends were delighted with the result and subjected the Pandavs and Draupadi to gross and terrible humiliation. Ill omens pervaded the skies and even Dhritarashtr was filled with shame and remorse over the goings-on in the royal assembly. Upon his insistence—and despite the resistance to this from Duryodhan—their kingdom and freedom were returned to the Pandavs. Yudhishthir should have walked away. But he did not.

The Kaurav side asked for a rematch; Yudhisthir once again walked into the same trap. The Pandavs lost—again. As per the agreed conditions of the game, the Pandavs had to accept exile for twelve years and remain incognito for a thirteenth year; were their identities discovered before the thirteenth year was up, the twelve-year exile would begin again. If they survived the thirteen years, they could return and have their kingdom restored to them. The rule-abiding

Pandavs, even while knowing that Shakuni and Duryodhan had cheated in the dice game, accepted these harsh conditions. They used the exile to improve themselves: they learnt new skills, acquired celestial weapons, and built powerful friendships and alliances.

At the end of the thirteenth year, the Pandavs and Draupadi returned to Hastinapur, with the expectation that their kingdom would be duly returned to them. Duryodhan, however, refused to keep his side of the bargain. Krishn tried to mediate between the two sides but to no avail. Even after Yudhishthir offered that he and his brothers would be satisfied with just five villages, Duryodhan declared:

यावद्धि तीक्ष्णया सूच्या विध्येदग्रेण केशव ।
तावदप्यपरित्याज्यं भूमेर्नः पाण्डवान् प्रति ॥

(Yavaddhi tikshanaya soochya vidhyedagreyna Keshav
Taavadyaparityaajyam bhoomernaha pandavan prati.)

No land shall we surrender to the Pandavs, not even that which can be pierced by the point of a needle.

—Mahabharat, V. 127. 25

The war, which many had tried to prevent and delay, was now imminent. Both sides turned to Krishn for help. Krishn, in a spirit of fairness and not wishing Arjun or Duryodhan (emissaries of the two sides) to leave empty-handed, made them an offer. One side could have Krishn's huge army of valiant fighters with all their weaponry. The

other side could have Krishn, albeit with an important
caveat: Krishn would be alone, and he would not fight
in the war. Arjun, without the slightest hesitation, chose
Krishn; Duryodhan was just as delighted with the deal
that he had received. Both believed that they had secured
the better part of the bargain.

The two armies faced each other at Kurukshetr and
turned out to be evenly matched. On the Kaurav side
were some of the most accomplished warriors: Bhishm,
Dronaacharya, Kripaacharya, Ashwatthama, Karn and
the many Kaurav princes. The Pandav side was also
formidable with the five princes and their allies. Lord
Krishn agreed to serve as Arjun's charioteer. Conch-shells
blew. But just before the charge began, Arjun was struck
by profound moral doubt: what pleasure could there
possibly be in killing one's own kith and kin? He laid
down his bow and arrow and said, 'I will not fight.' On
this same battlefield then, Lord Krishn delivered to Arjun
the sermon of the Bhagavad Gita—the Divine Song. This
remarkable text contains some of the most profound
insights of Hindu philosophy. It is also a call to action—
and not action for its own sake but righteous action.
Krishn patiently answered Arjun's questions, addressed
all his doubts and revealed his divine form, which is
described in the following words:

दिवि सूर्यसहस्रस्य भवेद्युगपदुत्थिता ।
यदि भा: सदृशी सा स्याद्भासस्तस्य महात्मन: ॥

(Divi sooryasahatrasya bhavedyugpadutthitaa
Yadi bhaahaa sadrishi saa syaadbhaasastasyaa
mahatmanaha.)

*If the light of a thousand suns were to be
simultaneously ablaze in the sky,
Even their splendour would not match the glory of that
great form of the divine.*

—Bhagavad Gita, 11.12

The discourse continues for eighteen chapters. At the end of the exchange, Arjun's doubts were dispelled. He arose with confidence, and the battle began.

The war lasted for eighteen days. Both sides resorted to deceit and betrayal, violating some of the most basic laws of war. The Pandav side won, but only after both sides had incurred terrible losses. Arjun's sixteen-year-old son, Abhimanyu, fought single-handedly against the Kaurav greats (including Dronaacharya, who should have known better) in the Chakravyuha formation, and was brutally killed; Ashwatthama crept into the Pandav camp in the dark of the night and mercilessly murdered everyone there (including women, children and the wounded). The Pandavs also showed scarce compassion or morality. Karn was slain by Arjun—on Krishn's urging—when he was unarmed; Dronaacharya was killed by the hand of Drishtadyumn, but in fact by the falsely spoken word of Yudhishthir, who announced the fake news of Ashwatthama's death in order to destroy the great teacher's spirit; Bhishm, who could not be killed by any man, was shot fatally when a barrage of arrows rained on him, unleashed by Arjun who used Shikhandi as a shield (who had previously been Amba, a woman who had vowed to destroy Bhishm and conducted years of penance towards this); Duryodhan too met a treacherous end, struck below the belt by Bheem's mace. On the Kaurav side, there were only three survivors: Kripaacharya, Kritavarman and the unfortunate Ashwatthama, who was cursed to wander the earth for eternity with wounds that would never heal. The Pandav side, although victorious, was also greatly destroyed, with only a handful of heroes surviving.

Yudhisthir was duly crowned king. An era of peace followed under his reign. Krishn was cursed by Gandhari for not having done enough to stop the carnage: his Yaadav clan would be struck by in-fighting just as had afflicted the Bharat dynasty, and Krishn himself would die a sorry death, being mistaken for a deer by a hunter. With the passage of time, the Pandavs and Draupadi also found their powers fading. They decided to abandon their worldly lives and proceeded to the forest to embrace a life of renunciation, followed by a final journey—*mahaprasthaan*—towards heaven.

On this trying and long voyage, they were accompanied by a dog. The travellers, each one for their various sins and transgressions, collapsed on the way. Ultimately, only Yudhishthir and his canine companion were left, and together they arrived at the gates of heaven. Indr, the king of gods, invited Yudhishthir to join him on the celestial chariot but insisted that the dog should be left behind. A debate followed, with Yudhishthir choosing to decline paradise rather than abandon his faithful friend. The dog, in fact, was Dharm—Yudhishthir's father—who now revealed his true form. Yudhishthir had passed the final test; he was greeted with honour and reunited with his family.

The structure of the Mahabharat

I	Aadiparv	History of the Bharat dynasty, early years of training, and the making of the Kaurav and Pandav warriors.
II	Sabhaaparv	The ugly politics of the royal assembly.
III	Vanaparv/Aaranyakparv	The twelve years of Pandav exile.
IV	Viraatparv	The thirteenth year spent incognito by the Pandavs.
V	Udyogparv	Efforts to avoid war.
VI	Bhishmaparv	War begins; the first ten days of the Kurukshetr war, with Bhishm serving as commander of the Kaurav army; includes the sermon of the Bhagavad Gita by Lord Krishn to Arjun at the start of the war.
VII	Dronparv	Days eleven to fifteen of the war, with Dronaacharya as commander of the Kaurav army.
VIII	Karnparv	Days sixteen and seventeen of the war, with the Kaurav army under the command of Karn.
IX	Shalyaparv	Day eighteen of the war, with the Kaurav army under the command of Shalya; the war ends.

X	Sauptikparv	Ashwatthama, Kritavarma and Kripaacharya inflict revenge by attacking the sleeping Pandav camp in the night.
XI	Streeparv	Lamentations by the women on the terrible destruction.
XII	Shantiparv	A disillusioned Yudhishthir is crowned king; Bhishm, on his deathbed, offers vital insights on kingship, governance and law.
XIII	Anushaasanparv	Bhishm's teachings to Yudhishthir on a wide range of issues, including the importance of compassion and non-violence.
XIV	Ashwamedhikaparv	The unification of the kingdom under the Pandavs.
XV	Aashramvasikaparv	Renunciation of the worldly life and departure to the forest by the elders.
XVI	Mausalaparv	The destruction of Krishn's clan through in-fighting.
XVII	Mahaaprasthaanikaparv	The final journey of the Pandavs.
XVIII	Swaragaarohanparv	Yudhishthir's test and ascent to heaven.

3

On Alliances and Partnerships: Ganesh, Vyaas and the Writing of the Mahabharat

अलंकृतं शुभैः शब्दैः समयैर्दिव्यमानुषैः ।
छन्दोवृत्तैश्च विविधैरन्वितं विदुषां प्रियम् ॥

(Alankritam shubhaihi shabdaihi
samayairdivyamanushaihi
Chhandovrittaishcha vividhairanvitam
vidushaam priyam.)

*The epic poem is adorned with auspicious words, at
times divine, at times human
Its rhymes and metres are dear to the learned . . .*

—Mahabharat I.1.28

The great sage Ved Vyaas was amongst the wisest. Having learnt from the ancient scriptures and having immersed himself in oral traditions, he had composed an epic poem on the history of the Bharatas. This auspicious poem was adorned with a treasure of perfectly strung together words, demonstrated great skill with poetic metres, and contained within it the secrets of the Vedic texts and the essence of all other sacred and secular texts. It spanned a diversity of disciplines. Its topics ranged from war strategy, diplomacy and architecture to all the ethical and pragmatic guidance that a person would need to live a fulfilled life. The mysteries of the past, present and future lived in it.

Vyaas was now in deep reflection. The enormous poem was ready in his head, but how should he make it accessible to other scholars, students and the public at large? Brahma, the creator, learnt of Vyaas's concern and visited him at his hermitage. Recognizing the complexity, encompassing character and profound wisdom the poem entailed, he gave Vyaas the following advice: No human is capable of penning this great work; you should meditate upon Lord Ganesh and ask for his help, for he alone will be able to perform this superhuman feat.

The sage followed Brahma's advice and meditated on Ganesh—the elephant-headed god, remover of obstacles, the first to be worshipped, and patron of artistic and intellectual enterprises—who answered his prayers and arrived immediately. Vyaas then put forth his request: he had composed a poem, and all that remained to be done was to dictate it to a worthy scribe. Would Ganesh take on this role?

Ganesh was inclined to agree, but not without some conditions that would test the nerve, grit and ability of the poet. He responded: I will take on this task as long as your dictation is unbroken, for my pen must flow smoothly and continuously to serve this purpose.

Vyaas knew right away that this condition was no laughing matter. To dictate a poem (comprising tens of thousands of verses) without stopping would be impossible—even he, as its composer, would need time to catch his breath, reconsider parts of the composition and rethink his next steps. Besides, Ganesh was the god of all intellectual pursuits—how could Vyaas possibly keep up with a scribe of such swift and sharp intelligence? He discerned that he could not agree to the condition but also did not want to lose the opportunity to work with this divine and magnanimous scribe. And so, Vyaas put forth his own condition: he would agree, but Ganesh must not write anything unless he had fully understood the content of the dictation.

व्यासोऽप्युवाच तं देवमबुद्ध्वा मा लिख क्वचित् ।
ओमित्युक्त्वा गणेशोऽपि बभूव किल लेखकः ॥

(Vyaasoapyuvacha tam devamabuddhaa ma
likh kvachit
Om itiuktva Ganeshoapi babhoova kil lekhakaha.)

Vyaas also then said, without understanding the
meaning, you must not write anything.
Ganesh then uttered the sound of 'Om'
(believed to be the origin of all creation), accepted the
condition and became the scribe.

—Mahabharat, I.1.79

And thus began the mammoth task of writing the great
Indian epic, with this remarkable duo working hand in
hand: one human, the other divine, one reciting the verses,
the other taking down the dictation. Whenever Vyaas
needed a breather, he would inject complexity and double
meaning into his verses. Even Ganesh—despite being the
most intelligent of all the gods—would need time and effort
to disentangle the mysteries of such verses; this he duly did,
driven both by a genuine curiosity and to keep his end of
the bargain. Except for these occasions, Ganesh's pen flew
across the pages. So swiftly did he write that his pen broke.
Legend has it that Ganesh, without giving the matter a
second thought, then simply broke off his right tusk to use
as a pen. Even today, most images of Lord Ganesh depict
him with a broken tusk, reminding us of the extraordinary
teamwork that made the Mahabharat.

Lessons for the every day

The collaboration between one of the wisest of sages and a god may seem rather distant from the humdrum of our daily lives at first glance. Take a second look though, and we have before us a wonderful exercise in fellowship and camaraderie, which remains as relevant for us today as it was in the historical and mythical domains of the Mahabharat.

First and foremost, the story highlights the importance of teamwork. There are some tasks that simply cannot be performed alone. Perhaps it is not surprising that most management manuals make ready reference to this, and job interviewers and interviewees prioritize this as a quality for appointments at different levels.

Second, the story offers another important insight that is sometimes omitted amidst the emphasis on teamwork: whom you choose to team up with matters as much as the teamwork itself. Brahma's advice to Vyaas, for instance, was that only the god of intelligence and creativity—Ganesh himself—would be up to the challenge of penning the Mahabharat. When Vyaas entreated Ganesh to become the scribe for his poem, he knew full well that his request might be refused. He tried nonetheless, for Ganesh was known to be generous and kind. Even if Ganesh had declined, there would have been neither shame for Vyaas, nor strategic misuse of Vyaas's need by so noble an interlocutor. The poet Kalidas captured this insight beautifully in his poem, *Meghadoot*:

याञ्चा मोघा वरमधिगुणे नाधमे लब्धकामा ।

(Yaancha mogha varamadhigune naadhame
labdhakaamaa.)

*A favour asked of an honourable person, even if
rejected, is superior to one that is granted by a
wicked person.*

—*Meghadoot*, Poorvamegh, 6

The second lesson of the story is thus: choose your team members wisely. Teamwork matters, but it needs worthy team players. Ill-chosen team members can sabotage projects and damage team spirit much more than outsiders can. For instance, Karn chose Shalya as his charioteer for the war; this was unwise, for Shalya's loyalties were known to lie with the Pandavs, and he used every opportunity he could find to destroy Karn's morale on the battlefield. Hence, although teamwork is of great value, it can only be done with trustworthy colleagues (or open-minded colleagues with whom trust can be built). If there is doubt, it is better to go it alone (and redefine the task itself), rather than team up with a player who is fundamentally ill-disposed towards you or your endeavour. This caution is also essential if one is an employer hiring new team players.

The third lesson is one on bargaining and negotiation. In some ways, the exchange between Vyaas and Ganesh was a highly asymmetric one. Vyaas was human, whereas Ganesh a god (and no minor deity at that). The fact that Ganesh was accepting his request at all may have led

Vyaas to accept whatever conditions the god might have chosen to impose. Interestingly though, when Ganesh put forth his condition, the sage was not intimidated. Instead, he came up with a counter-condition to ensure the deal would still work in his own favour, while also meeting Ganesh's condition. Of course, Ganesh was a uniquely intelligent and beneficent partner to negotiate with; in real life, one's counterparts may not always be so gracious. But the story remains an important one in demonstrating the value of bargaining and developing creative solutions rather than simply accepting what one is offered. It also reflects the deep-rooted democratic traditions of India, where deliberation, debate and argumentation transcended social hierarchies.

And a final point on the lessons that this story offers: in a way, the problem that Ved Vyaas faced was a rather modern one. How can one make one's works accessible to the right audience/a wider audience? Should the medium be a book, a paper, an op-ed, a blog? Is the message better conveyed in written, graphic or oral format? Are multimedia efforts suitable? One makes these choices partly based on the targeted audience. Having the blessing and support of Ganesh certainly helped Vyaas, both in the very important sense of encouragement and morale, and in terms of widening his reach. The latter is evident in the fact that even today, we celebrate this story of the origins of the great epic. Especially in an age when false narratives abound, dissemination of the message can be as important as the message itself. The value of allies in amplifying one's voice and getting one's message across should not be underestimated.

Lessons for foreign policy

For matters of diplomacy, statecraft and foreign policy too, the story offers some useful lessons.

First and foremost, the Ganesh–Vyaas collaboration is relevant for alliance-building, not only amongst individuals but also amongst states. There are some tasks that simply cannot be performed alone. For instance, recent years have seen the misuse of economic interdependence for geopolitical purposes.[1] Authoritarian states—with state-owned enterprises that are beholden to share data of global consumers (if asked by their government)—may be able to hold democracies hostage via control over hubs of deeply integrated supply chains, especially in strategically important sectors (e.g. energy, infrastructure, pharmaceutical). The answer to this, however, is not self-reliance, isolationism and deglobalization, which may produce short-term security but at the cost of economic growth and development. Rather, the answer lies in realigned supply chains. This calls for rewritten rules of trade multilateralism, which allow deeper integration with like-minded allies as well as the ramping up of domestic production capacities. In this new form of globalization, closer partnerships and alliances, which transcend economic and security divides, will be far more important than in the old, universal form of globalization.[2]

Second, even amongst friends, bargaining and negotiation may be necessary, and should be embraced as such. This applies even more to matters of high politics and statecraft, when leaders are not acting for themselves but to represent the interests of their peoples. While working with apparently more powerful allies, we do not have to accept all the terms that are meted out to us. India's resistance to being pressured by the West to change its position on the Russian invasion of Ukraine is a good example of this.

Third, being solution-oriented is important, and more so when dealing with allies rather than rivals. Instead of simply rejecting Ganesh's condition as unreasonable, Vyaas played a more positive game: he added his own condition. A deal resulted that not only allowed face-saving for both sides but also worked in content for the two players. Together, they were able to achieve their shared goal; the resulting product turned out to be a public good that has survived through millennia and travelled across different parts of the world. This is the stuff that international cooperation is—or should be—made of.

To apply these lessons, let us continue with the Russia–Ukraine case, taking into account the persistent attempts by European leaders to persuade India to condemn Russia as well as join their sanctions' efforts.[3] What could the next steps be? Similar to Ganesh and Vyaas working together, a constructive solution needs to be sought. Were Western powers to recognize India's constraints on this matter, both sides would be better served, as would the cause of democracy in the medium-run. Instead of lecturing to India, they could assist the world's largest democracy in the diversification of its military dependence away from Russia. And taking a page out of the same book, Europe could deepen economic cooperation with India to reduce its own over-dependence on China. India, in turn, could go beyond its (often legitimate) finger-pointing at Western hypocrisy and instead highlight the geo-economic gains to be had were Europe to deepen strategic cooperation with democratic India.

European Union (EU)–India trade relations provide another terrain for us to apply the lessons of the Ganesh–Vyaas story. Negotiations over the EU–India Free Trade Agreement began in 2007 but had to be put on hold in 2013 due to 'a gap in ambition'.[4] It took almost a decade to relaunch the negotiations in 2022. Difficulties are likely to persist over a host of fundamental disagreements: for instance, India will still be reluctant to accept the EU's labour and environmental standards, and both sides have different reasons for protectionism in their agricultural and manufacturing sectors. Despite all the goodwill, the negotiations could stall again if the two stick to their positions. A way to keep the negotiations going in order to achieve a mutually acceptable and long-lasting agreement would be—akin to Vyaas's bargain with Ganesh—to alter the frame with a new parameter. Were the agreement to be framed not purely as a narrow 'trade' agreement, but one with larger implications—with respect to geo-economic/security concerns—the urgency of a deal would become more apparent. Effectively placed frames and carefully built narratives that focus on the necessity of this bilateral cooperation amidst changing security imperatives could have a positive impact on some of the obvious, trade-related problems. It could lead the EU to soften its traditionally hard line on its more traditional non-trade concerns (such as social standards); India too may be more willing to meet the EU halfway on issues such as animal welfare and climate change (where it had taken seemingly obstructionist positions in the past but could now 'own' under the environmentalist causes espoused under Prime Minister Narendra Modi's leadership).[5]

Above all, the negotiation between Ganesh and Vyaas shows the importance of mutual respect, which can help resolve disagreement amongst parties who are well-disposed to each other. Neither Ganesh nor Vyaas took the other for granted. Both were invested in a shared goal and showed themselves willing to reframe the negotiation space to achieve this. This may intuitively seem like the obvious thing to do. But states sometimes make it much harder for themselves when negotiating with like-minded partners because they fail to sufficiently value the support of friendly states.[6] We draw on stories from the Mahabharat in later chapters, which show that a very different negotiation approach may be needed when dealing with hostile parties. At this point though, suffice it to note that allies are crucial to certain types of endeavours; negotiation amongst friends is acceptable, sometimes even necessary; and mutually respectful and creative bargaining can strengthen the relationship.

4

On Focus and the Big Picture: The Accuracy of Arjun's Aim

भासं पश्यसि यद्येनं तथा ब्रूहि पुनर्वचः ।
शिरः पश्यामि भासस्य न गात्रमिति सोऽब्रवीत् ॥

(Bhaasam pashyasi yadyenam tatha broohi
punarvachaha
Shiraha pashyaami bhaasasya na gaatramiti
soabraveet.)

*If you see the bird, describe its features to me (said
Dronaacharya)
(Arjun replied) I see only the head of the bird, I do not
see the body of the bird.*

—Mahabharat, I.132.7

39

The core message of this story is a much loved one in India. We recount it now with all the exquisite embellishments it comes with, and with much affection as it is a story that we were all introduced to in childhood by parents and grandparents. Importantly, the story has two parts, with the first part being the better known. Here, we also present the second part of the story, and explain why the two deserve to be read together.

One day, Guru Dronaacharya decided to test the skills of his pupils. The princes had learnt the techniques of using many powerful weapons, but the great teacher wished to now examine how they applied this knowledge as per their individual temperaments and in response to different situations. Towards this, Dronaacharya had a bird made of clay set up on the branch of a tree. He then told his students that he would ask each of them, one by one, to try to shoot the clay bird using a bow and arrow, with the aim of decapitating it in a single shot.

Yudhishthir was the first to be invited to the challenge. Dronaacharya said to Yudhishthir, 'Oh courageous one, mount your arrow upon your bow; at my signal, release the shaft.' Inspired by his teacher's words, Yudhishthir, the tormentor of foes, readied himself and his weapon

and stood poised to shoot. After a short pause, the
teacher asked his student to focus his eye on the bird
seated in the tree; Yudhishthir responded that he saw
the bird clearly. Yet another pause later, Dronaacharya
asked the eldest Pandav, 'Do you also see the tree,
your brothers and me?' Yudhishthir's response was in
the affirmative: indeed, he saw the tree, his brothers
and his teacher. His eager response, however, did not
please Dronaacharya. With some irritation, stating that
Yudhishthir would not be able to pierce the mark, he
sent the eldest of the Pandav brothers back to his seat
amongst the other pupils.

Each one of the students was then invited to perform
the task. Duryodhan responded to the teacher's questions
in much the same way as Yudhishthir had done; he too was
chided and dispatched back to the group. In fact, all the
Kaurav and Pandav brothers, as well as the other princes
who were learning from the famous warrior-teacher
responded with a 'yes': they could see all the things that
Dronaacharya mentioned in his questions. Each prince was
then dismissed by the disappointed teacher, without being
allowed to fire the arrow. All but one.

Finally, it was Arjun's turn. Dronaacharya now smiled
and said to him: 'Your task is to pierce the head of this bird
with your bow and arrow. Take a good look at the target.
When I give you the signal, you must shoot. Draw your
bow and prepare your aim.'

Arjun adopted the needed stance and took aim. His
bow was so tightly drawn that it almost took the shape of
a circle. After a short pause, Dronaacharya addressed him
with the question: 'Arjun, do you see the tree on which the
bird sits, and do you see me?' Arjun's answer was clear

and prompt: 'Sir, I see only the bird. I do not see the tree or you.' After another short interval, Dronaacharya asked Arjun, 'Son, as you look at the bird, can you describe its features to me?' Arjun replied,

'शिरः पश्यामि भासस्य न गात्रमिति ।'

(Shiraha pashyaami bhaasasya na gaatramiti.)

'I see only the head of the bird, I do not see the rest of its body.'

—Mahabharat, I.132.7

Dronaacharya was delighted with Arjun's answer. Joyously he cried, 'Fire your arrow!' This Arjun did without a second thought. His arrow was swift, sharp and precise. As expected, it did not miss its mark, and the head of the clay bird fell to the ground. Dronaacharya embraced Arjun, impressed with the proven excellence of his star pupil.

This story is often cited to teach students the importance of focus and concentration. But contrary to common belief, it does not stop here.

With the test completed, the entire party went to the river Ganga for a swim. A powerful water-beast, swimming underwater, caught hold of Dronaacharya's leg. As a highly accomplished warrior, Dronaacharya was perfectly capable of defending himself. But he decided to use the occasion as a real-life test for his students and called out for their help. While all the other pupils were thrown into confusion, Arjun responded swiftly. He shot five fierce arrows into the water and killed the creature. Dronaacharya was now fully convinced of Arjun's reflexes, technical skills and exceptional control of his senses. He endowed Arjun with a weapon whose extraordinary strength had been spoken of in all three worlds—the Brahmashir, which was to be used only against a demonic foe in battle; were it used casually against a weak human, it could destroy all creation. Arjun pledged to follow his guru's instructions, accepted the weapon and bowed to his teacher. Dronaacharya promised that in archery, Arjun would have no equal.

Lessons for the every day

In a famous poem, 'The Scholar-Gypsy', Victorian poet Matthew Arnold captured the human condition in the following words:

> Before this strange disease of modern life,
> With its sick hurry, its divided aims,
> Its heads o'ertax'd, its palsied hearts . . .[1]

Arnold's words ring truer than ever today, in our world of social media, relentless demands on our time and multiple distractions. Through much of our everyday lives, we flit mindlessly from task to task, just as we sometimes sit exhausted in front of our televisions meaninglessly changing channels or purposelessly scrolling through our social networking accounts. Other kinds of 'noise' also impede us from reaching goals that we truly value. Against this backdrop, Arjun's performance offers some inspiring lessons. It demonstrates how effective the power of concentration can be. It is possible that some of his siblings and cousins might have been technically as skilled as Arjun was. But via his single-minded purpose, Arjun came to surpass all other archers.

Arjun's mindful concentration is a useful exemplar to follow not only as a daily practice but also applies to challenging occasions in which one is put to the test. These include situations of formal learning but also others that we encounter in the course of our professional lives. Especially when tough decisions are to be made, there is a plethora of views and opinions available, as well as pressures being exercised. When faced with such situations, it is extremely important to be able to focus on the goal at hand.

While the first part of the story—of Arjun's precise aim at the clay bird—highlights the importance of being able to drown out the noise and focus on the goal, the second part offers a further lesson. When Dronaacharya called out for help, all the other students were caught off guard; Arjun was the only one who remained calm and collected and was thus able to put his skills to effective and timely use. Urgent crises demand a rapid assessment of the context, and then swift and precise action.

We believe that reading the two episodes together gives a better and more complete formula for action because they highlight the importance of balance between two seemingly contradictory approaches. Arjun's capacity to crowd out irrelevant distractions is the lesson of the first part; this ability was a necessary condition for ensuring the unfailing accuracy of his aim. But even the greatest exactness of aim, on its own, would not have sufficed under the conditions of existential danger and rampant confusion described in the second part.

When his teacher's life appeared to be in peril, Arjun was able to adapt his skills to this demanding context. In contrast to the first episode, our brave archer did not have the opportunity to pace himself and thereby slowly but surely focus his aim; rather, immediate action was required. Also in contrast to the demonstration in class, this time Arjun had to swiftly grasp the context, while also ignoring the panic and commotion amongst his classmates as they all saw their teacher come under attack from an unseen beast of the deep. This included estimating the depth of the water, assessing the size and movement of the monster, and ensuring Dronaacharya was not injured via a misfired shot. It was not only his deep concentration, but indeed his ability to take into account the *relevant* details of context that empowered Arjun to take the required and timely action. Yes, focus is important. But the ability to grasp and adapt to changing external conditions and then apply that single-minded focus amidst tough time constraints are just as important.

Imagine yourself taking an examination as a student. You could, single-mindedly as Arjun did in part one of the story, focus on one question and write the perfect answer. But you would not do well in that exam without reading the instructions on top: is this an examination that requires you to answer all eight questions, or choose two from the eight, or is it really a single-question examination? You would also be well served to keep an eye on the context, e.g. how should you divide your time? Included within the context would also be the subject in which you are being examined: an essay on the topic of 'infinity', for instance, would require very different content depending on whether the assessment is in the field of physics versus philosophy versus poetics.

Take the two parts of the story together, and the message is clear: to excel, specifics matter, but so does the big picture.

Lessons for governance and foreign policy

The episode, in its entirety, is relevant for public and foreign policy.

The first part of the story—focused aim—is perhaps one of the hardest ones for policymakers and politicians to emulate. Managing the political economy of diverse interests and ideas, which are, in turn, filtered through various bureaucratic institutions, is not an exercise that allows for single-minded purpose. At best, circles are somehow squared to reach uncomfortable and delicate compromises; more often than not (and as many of our friends in the world of policy readily admit), there is a default practice of somehow 'muddling through'. Democracies, for all their many, incomparable virtues, are especially prone to this problem.

European governments, for instance, are amongst the highest ranked in the Environmental Performance Index 2022,[2] commendably showing a commitment to green policies. Ironically, however, these same governments are often amongst the most generous in terms of public spending on families with children (including cash transfers),[3] as well as other forms of support (such as parental leave programmes),[4] thereby incentivizing population growth on an already deeply overburdened planet. In other words, environmental policies and social policies tend to be out of sync. We see a similar policy incoherence as epitomized in the EU's mantra of China being a 'partner, competitor and rival'. This formulation, in effect, allows for an 'anything goes' menu of strategies (instead of a coherent and clear set of instruments to deal with an increasingly powerful and adventurist China). The German chancellor Olaf Scholz has also shown himself to be prey to this problem. Despite his courageous announcement of a *Zeitenwende* (epochal change), his actions remain rather similar to those of his predecessor, Angela Merkel. This is reflected in the willingness of the German government to deepen trade and investment relations with China, including in critical infrastructure (for instance, by allowing a Chinese shipping company to acquire stakes in a container terminal at the port of Hamburg).

The solution to these problems lies in prioritization, just as Arjun was able to focus his mind and eye on the relevant detail while ignoring all other irrelevant ones. This is of course easier said than done, and much depends on the type of leaders as well as political institutions (for instance, parliamentary and federal systems are likely to find it harder to achieve policy coherence in comparison to presidential and centralized systems). But difficult does not mean impossible. Having a well-defined grand strategy (embodied in a national security strategy, for instance) is a useful step towards achieving policy coherence. Differentiation between first-order, non-negotiable goals of principle versus second-order goals can assist in the prioritization process. For instance, were a government to commit to environmental preservation as a first-order goal, this would require and enable political choices that align social policies with green priorities. Similarly, if national security were treated as a first-order goal of national existence, then economic policy would have to be treated as a part of this (rather than as a sole priority in its own right). But in matters of high politics too, the lessons of the second part of Arjun's story deserve to accompany the first.

After core goals are prioritized (which requires the filtering out of clearly identified secondary goals[5]) and policy is targeted towards achieving them, it is just as important to keep a close eye on context. In the case of foreign policy, this requires a willingness to make key strategic decisions that may require a reversal of some previous strategies. For instance, India's enthusiastic commitment to the BRICS grouping (Brazil, Russia, India, China and South Africa) may have made sense when the group was founded (in 2009) and the rising powers shared an economic agenda. It makes lesser sense in the context of the security threat that China now poses to India (as well as considering the major incidents of armed conflict between the two countries in recent years). Similarly, India would be now well served to diversify its economy towards the West and reduce its dependence on China. The goal— of preserving India's autonomy and sovereignty—remains unchanged; the government needs to stay focused on this goal and simultaneously update its strategic and economic partnerships to align with the altered geopolitical and geo-economic context.

Arjun showed single-minded purpose to reach his goal, as well as adaptability of strategy to achieve it. In this special combination lies a key to success in much of what we do.

5

On Friendships That Transcend Social Barriers: Duryodhan and Karn

आचार्य त्रिविधा योनी राज्ञां शास्त्रविनिश्चये ।
सत्कुलीनश्च शूरश्च यश्च सेनां प्रकर्षति ॥

(Acharya trividhaa yoni raagyaam shaastravinishchaye
Satkuleenashcha shoorashcha yashcha senaam
prakarshati.)

*Oh great teacher, our sacred texts are clear that kings
have three origins:
Birth in a noble family, display of courage and service
as commander-in-chief.*

—Mahabharat, I.135.35

As the Kaurav and Pandav cousins came to complete their education in the martial arts, a tournament was organized where they—and any other warriors—could display their skills before their respected teachers, illustrious families and members of the public. In a grand arena, the brave young warriors engaged in sporting combat in different styles, as well as with a variety of weapons: swords, bows and arrows, clubs and more. Both sides were well matched, and public opinion was evenly divided on whether the Kaurav or the Pandav brothers were the more skilled fighters. The only exception was Arjun. His chosen weapon was the bow and arrow; here, his skill was matchless, and he could harness the elements of fire, water and wind to his advantage. But he also showed himself to be highly accomplished with the sword, the club and a range of other arms.

Suddenly, at the entrance of the games arena, there was a sound as if bolts of lightning had struck against each other, as if mountains were exploding or as if the earth were tearing itself apart. In fact, this was the sound of a powerful man clapping his hand on his arm, flexing his muscles. The stranger who had emanated this sound was exceedingly handsome, golden like the sun, tall as a mountain, sporting a divine armour and earrings (which he had in fact been born with). In his hand he bore a bow, at his waist dangled a sword. As he walked in, it seemed as if a colossal and magnificent mountain were entering the marquee. This handsome stranger was Karn—son of Surya, the sun god—and his demeanour exuded the same splendour as his father's. The spectators were enamoured by his majestic presence and could not take their eyes off him.

Karn addressed Arjun in a deep and solemn voice: 'Oh son of Kunti, I can outperform you in all the skills that you have demonstrated; do not be arrogant in your victory.' The spectators gasped at so audacious a claim. Arjun, on being thus addressed, was embarrassed and angry. Duryodhan, however, was delighted and greeted the stranger with warmth. Karn thanked Duryodhan and requested that he be allowed to challenge Arjun to sole combat.

Arjun was unimpressed and spoke harshly: those who come uninvited and speak without being called upon to do so are lowly individuals who are deserving of a place in a special kind of hell; soon this impertinent stranger would be dispatched at Arjun's hands to this netherworld. Karn responded: the sports arena was meant for all people, why did Arjun imagine himself to have a special place in it? Such words were not becoming of a warrior but revealed Arjun's insecurities and weaknesses, argued Karn, and asked: Why not settle the matter with a duel? Arjun then readied himself for combat, as did Karn.

Kripaacharya, one of the esteemed teachers, then formally introduced Arjun to Karn as a son of Kunti and a jewel in the Kuru clan; he further asked the stranger to reveal to the assembly of which king he was born. Only after this information was provided could the duel begin, because princes could not fight those of ordinary birth or values. Karn, not being aware of his royal lineage and believing himself to be the son of a simple charioteer (who had adopted him after he was abandoned at birth), hung his head in shame upon being asked this question.

Duryodhan immediately came to the defence of the stranger. He argued the following:

आचार्य त्रिविधा योनी राज्ञां शास्त्रविनिश्चये ।
सत्कुलीनश्च शूरश्च यश्च सेनां प्रकर्शति ॥

(Acharya trividhaa yoni raagyaam shaastravinishchaye
Satkuleenashcha shoorashcha yashcha senaam
prakarshati.)

*Oh great teacher, our sacred texts are clear that kings
have three origins:
Birth in a noble family, display of courage and service
as commander-in-chief.*

—Mahabharat, I.135.35

Duryodhan's message was unambiguous: 'This stranger, on account of his great courage, is rightfully a king.' But Duryodhan did not stop there; he went further and showed his commitment to this idea via his actions. He stated, 'If Arjun still refuses to fight him on these grounds, then I herewith name and anoint the stranger as king of Angadesh.' And upon Duryodhan's instructions, priests immediately performed the necessary rituals and ceremonies, thereby crowning Karn the ruler of the kingdom of Angadesh.

Karn was moved beyond belief at Duryodhan's magnanimity and asked the Kaurav prince how he could repay him. Duryodhan reassured him that he desired nothing more than Karn's friendship. This, Karn promised him with all the sincerity and commitment that characterized his principled and noble nature.

A further incident followed, which cemented Karn's loyalty. Just after the crowning ceremony was completed, Karn's kindly, adoptive father arrived in the games arena. His attire was humble and old age had weakened him. Tears running down his face, he greeted his son with joy; Karn rushed down from his new throne to bow to him. Watching this sweet reunion of a proud father and his loving son touched the hearts of many but not of the Pandav brothers. Bheem now followed Arjun's suit and loudly ridiculed Karn: 'You are the son of a chariot driver—you don't even deserve death at Arjun's hand!'

At this point, the sun set, and the day's proceedings were brought to a close. The battle between Arjun and Karn would have to wait. But a powerful deal was already sealed, the consequences of which would reverberate through the decades. Duryodhan's willingness to recognize talent beyond the divides of caste and class had won him his most loyal friend, ally and supporter. The Pandavs did not help themselves in this regard: while Duryodhan showed himself to be meritocratic, the Pandavs stuck firmly to elitist social mores. Duroyodhan offered Karn a kingship based on his bravery and skills, whereas Arjun and Bheem heaped insults and ridicule on him for his apparently low birth. Karn would forget neither the kindness that

Duryodhan had shown him, nor the cruel slights and slurs that he had received at the hands of Arjun and Bheem.

The time would come when Karn's loyalty would be severely tested. He would be tempted with the promise of an entire and united empire, primacy amongst the Pandav brothers as victor, a woman of great beauty and intelligence—Draupadi—as his wife, and above all, the prestige and social standing that he had yearned for all his life. His birth mother, Kunti, would embrace him and take responsibility for the many wrongs that had been inflicted on him. Even Lord Krishn would seek his hand in friendship and promise him all the material and spiritual gains he could wish for, and more. All these riches would be his, if only he would agree to switch sides from the Kaurav brothers to his real family, the Pandavs. And yet, Karn would readily forgo these enticements, sticking firmly and willingly by Duryodhan's side, just as he had promised on the day of the tournament.

Lessons for the every day

The story we have recounted here is not a popular one, perhaps because it portrays Duryodhan—usually the villain of the piece—in a rosy light, and the Pandav heroes, especially Arjun and Bheem, as narrow-minded, elitist and arrogant. Nonetheless, we have included it in this book because we wanted to highlight not only the black-and-whites of the text but also the greys. Perhaps the biggest difference between the two sides is that at a meta level, the Pandavs are really fighting for dharm, while the Kauravs are fighting purely for their self-interest. But if one observes the cousins not with a bird's-eye view but closer to the ground, the differences blur. Duryodhan and Karn are both complex and interesting characters who reveal much generosity, loyalty, kindness and open-mindedness. Equally, at different points in the text, the usually moral Pandavs also show themselves capable of fatal deception, wickedness and cruelty. In any case, we believe good lessons are to be learnt irrespective of whom they come from, heroes or villains. This story offers at least three useful lessons, which are applicable to the every day.

The first lesson is about sportsmanship. The Pandav side and even the great teachers of the Kuru clan tried to disqualify a promising competitor from the tournament by resorting to rules of caste and class. In doing so, they behaved in an unsportsmanlike fashion. In contrast, Duryodhan made the case that a courageous man was worthy of kingship; expecting resistance to this theoretical argument, he went on to act upon it by crowning Karn the king of Angadesh, and thereby firmly levelled the playing field between Arjun and Karn. Admittedly, Karn's challenge to Arjun would have pleased Duryodhan in the first place, and likely led him to be favourably inclined towards Karn. But in all that he did in this regard, Duryodhan acted single-handedly; he may have had the authority to do so, but he still showed moral courage by going against his teachers and elders. In sport and in real life, we can all stand up to ensure inclusiveness and fair play.

The second lesson is on the importance of seeing people for who they are and their potential, irrespective of titles. Karn was fortunate to have been blessed with a very attractive appearance, but his lack of a title was enough to disqualify him from the contest for the Pandav side as well as the elders in the congregation. Duryodhan, in contrast, chose not to get distracted by convention; instead, he saw potential in Karn and acted upon it. Sometimes, it is worth taking a chance on the apparent underdog.

The third and perhaps most important lesson of the story is how much damage exclusionary systems of caste and class can do. A foolish narrow-mindedness (that disregarded ability and prioritized social status) on the part of the wisest in the Kuru congregation reinforced the divisions between Karn and the other sons of Kunti. It is possible that Karn—a major protagonist in the great war— would have joined the side of dharm had he not had to frequently endure cheap jibes and public humiliation from the Pandav brothers on account of his seemingly low birth. The caste system in India is a shameful case in point, but the lack of social mobility and high barriers to people of colour in Western societies are also illustrative of this problem.[1] Merit and achievement can come in all shapes and sizes and deserve to be recognized and rewarded irrespective of where they come from.

Lessons for politics and foreign policy

The story offers several insights that are relevant to questions of governance as well as foreign policy.

In some ways, the treatment meted out to Karn by the great gurus and heroes of the congregation is reminiscent of how countries of the Global South are (even today) treated by the West. The anachronistic Permanent Five membership of the United Nations Security Council is an illustration of this: despite the fact that countries such as India, Brazil, South Africa and others have emerged as major players on the ground, not one of them has yet been welcomed as a member of a reformed High Table. Just as the great and the good in the story refused to update the rules, so also do we see a reluctance of the erstwhile Great Powers to update and reform membership criteria of old clubs. And the analogy does not end there.

The current overtures coming towards democracies, especially from the United States under the Biden administration, and to a lesser extent from Europe, suggest the making of a system of like-minded powers from the Global North and the Global South, which share core values. Look more closely, however, and there seems to be no dearth of hand-waving and finger-pointing on 'democratic backsliding' in the developing world, which come from researchers and policymakers (often from the Global North). Intellectual debates on liberalism usually do not allow for the possibility that there may be variants of liberalism that not only predate Western versions but may actually be even more liberal than the supposed blueprints that were developed in Europe.[2] Western democracies still seem to see themselves as an elitist club, to which Southern countries will seldom be good enough to be welcomed into. Akin to the refusal of the Pandavs and the elders to recognize Karn for his own merit and achievements, the West seems too ready to put democracies in the Global South back into the box that they expect them to sit in.

This type of behaviour leads to a double whammy. First and foremost, it is unfair to democracies—old and new—in the Global South. Second, it also does a disservice to the Global North by creating a self-fulfilling prophecy: democracies that are repeatedly put in camps with authoritarian states are then tempted to indeed align/realign with non-democracies (which sometimes give them an easier time on norms and also sweeten their interactions via seemingly generous terms of investment, infrastructure support and more). Just as the exclusionary behaviour of the Pandavs cemented the alliance between Duryodhan and Karn, Western powers risk driving democracies in the Global South into the arms of non-democracies and authoritarian states. The persistent attractiveness of BRICS for India today, despite its concerns about China's adventurism in its neighbourhood, is an illustration of this; another was India's reluctance to criticize the Russian invasion of Ukraine, thereby ending up once again in the same corner as China.

Global governance institutions need a major update of their structures and processes to be both inclusive and effective; Western democracies need a serious reconsideration of the values that they claim to uphold, and how these values are defined. Democratic and pluralist polities (some with ancient traditions of argumentation and collective deliberation) from the Global South need to be treated with respect and as equals. Without this, there is a real risk that like-minded friends from the Global South will end up on the side of authoritarian strongmen, to the detriment of themselves as well as liberal democracies of the Global North.

6

On Values and Interests: The Magical Being of the Lake and Yudhishthir

धर्म एव हतो हन्ति धर्मो रक्षति रक्षितः ।
तस्माद् धर्मं न त्यजामि मा नो धर्मो हतोऽवधीत् ॥

(Dharm eva hato hanti dharmo rakshati rakshitaha
Tasmaad dharmam na tyajaami maa no dharmo
hatoavadheet.)

When destroyed, dharm itself destroys; dharm protects
those who guard it.
That is why I do not renounce dharm, lest we too are
killed in its destruction.

—Mahabharat, III.313.128

Having lost their kingdom in a game of loaded dice, the Pandav brothers and their wife, Draupadi, were sent into exile. During these twelve years (with the thirteenth having to be spent incognito), the heroes of the Mahabharat faced many ordeals and hardships. One such trial—which tested their courage and integrity—came from the magical being of the lake, a *yaksh*.

A deer had run off with the firewood of a sage, and the Pandav brothers gave chase to retrieve the wood. The deer was not to be found. The brothers, exhausted from their efforts, were thirsty. Hearing the calls of cranes, Nakul deduced that a water source was in the vicinity and was dispatched by Yudhishthir to fetch water.

The water source turned out to be a lake of crystal clarity, where Nakul observed many cranes. As he neared the water to satiate his thirst, a voice boomed seemingly from the skies: 'Do not dare to drink from this lake; I have a prior claim on it. Answer my questions first, son of Madri, and then take as much as you wish.' Nakul disregarded the warning, drank from the lake and fell lifeless to the ground.

After having waited for Nakul, Yudhishthir sent Sahadev to investigate what had become of his twin and complete the errand. Sahadev too did not heed the voice, despite seeing Nakul's dead body by the lake. He drank the water and met the same fate as his brother.

Concerned about the well-being of the younger Pandav brothers, Yudhishthir now sent Arjun, wielder of the mighty bow, to bring back Nakul and Sahadev and the much-needed water. Believing some foul play to be at work as he saw the lifeless bodies of his brothers, Arjun readied his weapons. Expecting a battle, he thought it wise to quench his thirst first. The voice boomed, issuing the same warning as it had done to his younger siblings. Arjun did not appreciate being thus threatened by an invisible opponent. He challenged the speaker to show himself, fired arrows into the sky and built a barrier of arrows around himself. The creature of the lake, however, remained undeterred, and repeated the warning; when Arjun nonetheless drank from the lake, he also met his death.

Yudhishthir then sent the strongest of the five brothers, Bheem, to discover what had happened and to fulfil the errand of bringing water. Bheem saw his dead brothers and deduced that a powerful yaksh or *rakshas* was responsible. Before taking any action, he too considered it prudent to replenish his strength by quenching his thirst, and thus repeated the fatal error that his brothers had made: he disregarded the warning, drank from the lake and died.

With all four of his brothers now mysteriously disappeared, Yudhishthir—the most moral and judicious of the brothers—advanced to the lake and saw the dead bodies. He wondered what deception or evil magic was at play that had taken his brave brothers—all matchless warriors—with not a mark of violence on their bodies. As he ventured to drink from the lake, the voice now declared itself to be that of a crane's and admitted that it was responsible for the deaths of the four brothers. And once again, it issued the same warning: no water was to be drunk until the thirsty traveller had answered his questions.

Yudhishthir responded with the gentle humility that characterized his being. He respectfully asked the voice if it would disclose its real identity. This, the speaker duly did. It declared itself to be a yaksh. And then the voice once again warned Yudhishthir that as the yaksh, his claim to the lake preceded those of any passers-by such as the Pandav brothers; if Yudhishthir wanted to drink from the lake, he would have to answer his questions or else suffer the same fate that had been meted out to his brothers.

Yudhishthir wisely agreed and answered the questions with care. The questions were tough and addressed the core of morality, politics, societal norms and more. The yaksh was impressed by his answers. He granted him permission to drink from the lake. He also offered to revive any one of Yudhishthir's brothers. Yudhishthir chose his half-brother Nakul (son of Madri). Upon being asked why he had not chosen Arjun or Bheem—sons of Kunti, like himself, and therefore his real brothers—he answered, 'धर्मो रक्षति रक्षितः' [Dharmo Rakshati Rakshitaha]. Explaining his choice, Yudhishthir argued that he could not and would not forsake dharm. To refrain from causing pain to others was the supreme dharm. Through his own survival, Kunti would at least have one son remaining; it was only fair that one of Madri's sons should live too.

So moved was the yaksh by Yudhishthir's commitment to values, and especially the primacy that he attached to abstaining from injury to others, that he rewarded him by restoring all the brothers back to life.

Lessons for the every day

The story of the exchange between Yudhishthir and the yaksh is a popular one, with its extracts still dotting Sanskrit syllabi for schoolchildren in India. Barring a few of his answers to the yaksh's riddles on social mores that make little sense now, most of the verses have a timeless and universal quality to them.

A particularly striking verse appears towards the end of the dialogue between the two protagonists. The yaksh asks, what is a noteworthy fact, worthy of discussion? Yudhishthir's answer is hard-hitting, and in some ways, remarkably modern:

अस्मिन्महामोहमये कटाहे सूर्याग्निना रात्रिदिवेन्धनेन ।
मासर्तुदर्वीपरिघट्टनेनभूतानि कालः पचतीति वार्ता ॥

(Asmin mahaamohamaye kataahe suryaaragninaa
ratridivendhenena
Maasartudarviparighattanenabhootaani kaalaha
pachateeiti vaarta.)

*This world is a frying pan, the sun is the fire, day and
night are the fuel,
The months and seasons are the spoon, with which
time is cooking us—this is a topic worth talking about.*

—Mahabharat, III.313.118

In this conversation with the yaksh, Yudhishthir looks reality coldly in the eye and comes up with astute observations

that we can relate to even today. But just as important is
the long-lasting wisdom that many of his replies contain.
Yudhishthir gives us not only trenchant descriptions of the
human condition but also provides us with valuable advice
on codes of conduct. Imagine his responses as aphorisms
delivered swiftly in a rapid-fire round of an experienced
quizmaster, with capsule-sized empirical observations and
normative insights.

For instance, the yaksh asks Yudhishthir: 'Who is
the invincible enemy, what is the incurable disease, what
characteristic makes a sage and what is the characteristic
of the ungodly?' Yudhishthir's response is swift and
precise: 'Anger is the invincible enemy, greed is the
incurable disease, consideration of the good of all beings
is the characteristic of a saintly person and cruelty is
the trait of the ungodly.' Other memorable aphorisms
include: 'A real bath involves cleansing the mind of
all impurities and real charity involves protecting all
creatures.' When asked, who is truly happy, Yudhishthir
reminds us that the simple pleasures of life are not to be
taken for granted or underestimated. He answers: 'One
who is able to cook a modest amount of food in his home,
is not in debt and is not required to wander abroad (in
search of a living), he is truly happy.' If we were to try
to follow the advice implicit in Yudhishthir's answers,
we could live more contented lives. Simultaneously, we
would be promoting the safety and well-being of our
fellow creatures.

Besides the content of Yudhishthir's answers, just as
important is the act of his engagement with the yaksh.
Unlike his brothers, he does not presume to have any right
on the waters of the lake; when the yaksh—in the guise of

a crane—announces his prior claim, he respects this and plays by the set rules to gain access to its pure waters. This respect for the environment—and for all the creatures who have at least as much right to it as we do—is the need of the day now.

Additionally, via his sense of fairness, Yudhishthir sets us some powerful examples to follow. For instance, by choosing his half-brother, Yudhishthir seeks to protect dharm; this wise choice wins him the reward of having the lives of all four of his brothers restored. This is an important takeaway. Yudhishthir shows us that doing the right thing is rewarding not only in its own right but also because it can turn out to be a winning strategy.

Lessons for politics and foreign policy

In terms of the practice of politics and foreign policy, Yudhishthir's encounter with the yaksh of the lake gives us three key insights.

First, the issue of the prior claim of the yaksh to the lake applies not only to how we regard nature in our individual dealings but also to how we update and renegotiate the rules of global governance and foreign policy. This applies in cases of stolen treasures (such as the Kohinoor) acquired by imperial powers. It extends to how we regard the claims of other species on the lands, seas and resources that we—as humans—exploit in the name of development, growth, tradition or entertainment. Human population growth, for instance, needs to be problematized much more than polarized conversations (caught between the racism of the extreme right and the political correctness of the liberal left) have allowed for.[1] And insofar as the earth is a shared entity that is grossly overburdened by both dramatically growing consumption levels in parts of the Global South (fuelled by a push for improved standards of living for large numbers of poor people) as well as huge per capita consumption of limited resources in the Global North, the responsibility of limiting population growth needs to also be shared.

Second, most of our models of governance (domestic and international) are anthropocentric. This limits our ability to recognize the prior claims of 'others'. Yudhisthir, in contrast, recognizes the right of other creatures (crane or yaksh) to the lake as trumping the human claims of his brothers and himself. Try to apply a similar perspective that accords equal dignity to non-human species as human ones, and it is clear that researchers need to engage in a fundamental rethink on existing theories: of growth versus degrowth, as well as what constitutes (human) rights and personhood, whose interests are represented (and also fail to be represented) even in the most democratic of political systems, and who speaks for the voiceless. Herein lie the seeds of an ambitious, interdisciplinary research programme which brings together development economics, political theory and jurisprudence.

Third, Yudhishthir's emphasis on धर्मो रक्षति रक्षितः—dharm protects those who protect it—helps us shed new light on a false dichotomy that is prevalent in many academic and policy debates on *interests* and *values*. There is no dearth of researchers arguing, for instance, that to deal with a rising China, the United States and other powers will be better served finding allies based on shared interests.[2] Powerful business lobbies as well as political leaders in Europe emphasize the importance of not jeopardizing high profits secured via the Chinese market and are quite willing—after paying some lip service—to look the other way as far as human rights (or indeed animal rights) are concerned. A slightly more refined version of this argument was *Wandel durch Handel* (literally: change through trade). It was assumed that by prioritizing economic interests via trade and increasing interconnectedness, it would also be possible to bring about political change and convergence over values.

Yudhishthir's discourse with the yaksh offers us quite a different perspective. Several layers of interpretation can accompany the profundity of the idea: dharm protects those who protect it. Specifically with reference to the oft assumed interests–values dichotomy, Yudhishthir's insight suggests that if we protect our values, our interests will also be protected. This could be partly because values and interests are reflexive, with one shaping the other in a continuous cycle. But Yudhishthir's धर्मो रक्षति रक्षितः seems to go further than that: if push comes to shove, it is values that should perhaps be protected first—and not only for their own sake, not only for the sake of principle, but *because* doing so can also help protect interests.

Applied to foreign policy, global governance and multilateralism, Yudhishthir's insight is significant. Its implications include a turning of a fundamental assumption of the post-war order on its head (that is, economic integration automatically leads to prosperity and also peace).[3] Instead, Yudhisthir's experience offers some very different policy prescriptions that are centred on the importance of values: not technocratic and economic drivers, but political and moral drivers for peace; not universal integration amongst diverse partners but deep integration amongst like-minded allies; not further opening of markets and freer flow of goods, but closer trade links with countries that share one's values.

Above all, and leaving aside all the intricacies of foreign policy, Yudhishthir's experience collapses the interest *versus* values dichotomy into one powerful lesson: sometimes, it pays to be good.

7

To War or Not to War:
The Bhagavad Gita[1]

हतो वा प्राप्स्यसि स्वर्गं जित्वा वा भोक्ष्यसे महीम् |
तस्मादुत्तिष्ठ कौन्तेय युद्धाय कृतनिश्चय: ||
सुखदु:खे समे कृत्वा लाभालाभौ जयाजयौ |
ततो युद्धाय युज्यस्व नैवं पापमवाप्स्यसि ||

(Hato vaa praapsyasi swargam jitvaa vaa
bhokshyase mahim
Tasmatuttishtha Kaunteya yuddhaaya
kritanishchayaha.
Sukhdukhe same kritvaa laabhaalabhau jayaajayau
Tato yuddhaaya yujyasva naivam paapamavaapsyasi.)

*If you die, you will attain heaven, if you win, you will
enjoy the fruits of this earth
Therefore, arise, son of Kunti, and fight with
determination.
Treat joy and sorrow, profit and loss, and victory and
defeat as just the same,
And thereafter engage in battle; and in so doing, you
will incur no sin.*

—Bhagavad Gita, 2.37–38

The Kaurav and Pandav armies faced each other on the battlefield of Kurukshetr. It was a sight to behold. On both sides stood brave warriors, magnificent in their regal splendour, armed with celestial weapons, ready to lay down their lives. The sound of conch shells, drums, bugles and horns thundered across the skies. Arjun asked Lord Krishn—now serving as his charioteer—to drive the chariot to the centre of the battlefield, where he could look upon those who wished to please the wicked son of Dhritarashtr and were ready to fight by his side. Krishn complied with his request. Arjun was shaken by what he saw.

On both sides, he observed respected elders, teachers, cousins and well-wishers—family and friends—now pitted against each other, to fight unto death. Arjun's body shuddered at this gruesome spectacle, his famous bow—Gandiv—slipped from his hand, and his heart was filled with sorrow. What happiness could be had from victory, kingdom, or indeed all worldly pleasures, if they were to accrue from killing one's own relatives, teachers and friends? The Kauravs were the aggressors; driven by greed, they were willing to inflict death and destruction upon their kinsmen. But Arjun had no wish to go down the sinful path that Duryodhan and his army

were embracing with such alacrity. The Pandav archer
thus announced, 'Better far, if the sons of Dhritarashtr,
equipped with their weapons, were to slay me, unarmed
and unresisting.' Besides, said Arjun, it was not clear to
him which was worse—to be conquered by the enemy,
or to conquer the enemy—for even after a victory over
the Kauravs, Arjun could not imagine the Pandavs would
have the will left to live after having performed such
heinous acts against noble elders and teachers. Trembling
with grief, his eyes filled with tears, his distress acute,
caught in an existential dilemma and with his duty
unclear, Arjun laid down his bow and arrows. He spoke
the words, 'न योत्स्य' [na yotsya, meaning: 'I will not fight'],
and thereafter became silent.

What followed was the sermon of the Bhagavad
Gita—the Divine Song—delivered by Lord Krishn to
Arjun. With patience, Krishn addressed the supreme
archer and answered all his questions. This exchange
contains some of the core and most profound teachings
of Hindu philosophy. The text teaches us a remarkable
mix of pragmatism and morality, and somehow manages
to reconcile their seeming contradictions. It is as much a
poem about the relationship between the individual and
the universe as it is about how we should treat all our
fellow creatures. In its pluralism on the multiple paths that
it presents to achieving one's duty, as well as its attention
to the rights and well-being of the individual (human and
non-human), the Bhagavad Gita may well be regarded as
one of the earliest and far-reaching expositions of liberal
thought. But for the purposes of this chapter we focus
specifically on the arguments that Krishn presented to
address Arjun's distress on the question of war.

Krishn's immediate reaction was to gently chide Arjun:
such unmanliness and delusion were unbecoming of the
brave warrior. But very quickly, Krishn recognized the depth
of Arjun's despair and the seriousness of the moral qualms
that afflicted his kind heart. He then systematically and
with great compassion presented four sets of arguments to
explain why Arjun's anguish was uncalled for: metaphysical,
relating to personal duty, ethical and political.

Krishn's argumentation

First, Krishn reassured Arjun that there was no reason to
fear death—neither for his loved ones, be they Kaurav or
Pandav, nor for himself. The wise mourn neither the living
nor the dead because the soul is immortal.

न जायते म्रियते वा कदाचिन्नायं भूत्वा भविता वा न भूयः ।
अजो नित्यः शाश्वतोऽयं पुराणो, न हन्यते हन्यमाने शरीरे ॥
...नैनं छिन्दन्ति शस्त्राणि नैनं दहति पावकः ।
न चैनं क्लेदयन्त्यापो न शोषयति मारुतः ॥

(Na jaayate mriyate vaa kadaachinnaayam bhootvaa
bhavitaa vaa na bhooyaha
Ajo nityaha shaashvatoayam puraano, na hanyate
hanyamaane shareere.
. . . nainam chhindanti shastraani nainam dahati
paavakaha
Na chainam kledayantyaapo na shoshayati marutaha.)

*The soul is neither born nor can it ever die, having
existed it can never cease to be
It is birthless, eternal, immortal and ancient, it cannot
be killed even when the body is destroyed...*

Weapons cannot pierce it, fire cannot burn it,
Water cannot wet it, and wind cannot dry it.

—Bhagavad Gita, 2.20, 2.23

This idea recurs through several other chapters of the Bhagavad Gita, as do the various routes through which one may achieve the full recognition and wide-ranging implications of this eternal truth. But the notion of the immortal soul also has direct implications for Arjun's dilemma regarding the war: if one understands that the soul is eternal and imperishable, then surely it is also clear that neither its death nor its destruction is possible. In other words, Arjun's grief was misguided and uncalled for.

Second, Krishn reminded Arjun of his duty. Arjun—through his entire existence—had been trained to be a warrior. To fight was his duty, his dharm. Krishn said:

स्वधर्ममपि चावेक्ष्य न विकम्पितुमर्हसि ।
धर्म्याद्धि युद्धाच्छ्रेयोऽन्यत्क्षत्रियस्य न विद्यते ॥

(Svadharmapi chaavekshya na vikampitumaharsi,
Dharmyaddhi yuddhaachhreyoanyatkshatriyasya
na vidyate.)

Considering your duty as a warrior, you should
not waver.
There is nothing better for a warrior than to fight for
truth/righteousness/dharm.

—Bhagavad Gita, 2.31

Besides, advised Krishn, it is better to perform one's own duty imperfectly and even die doing so (स्वधर्मे निधनं श्रेय:, svadharme nidhanam shreyaha, Bhagavad Gita, 3.35) rather than to follow the path of another. It was essential to be true to oneself, and for Arjun this meant fighting this war.

Then came the third argument: this was not just any war. The battle of Kurukshetr that the Pandavs and Kauravs were fighting was a *dharmyuddh*—a war of good against evil. So vile had been the crimes of the opposing side that their annihilation was inevitable:

ऋतेऽपि त्वां न भविष्यन्ति सर्वे येऽवस्थिता: प्रत्यनीकेषु योधा: ।

(Riteapi tvaam na bhavishanti sarveyeavasthitaha
pratyaneekeshu yoddhaha.)

Even without your participation, those warriors
gathered on the opposing side will cease to exist.

—Bhagavad Gita, 11.32

That the villains would eventually be brought to justice was not to be doubted. Arjun, through his whole-hearted contribution to the war effort, would simply be serving as an instrument of divine justice in hastening their end.[2]

Finally, there was a pragmatic—indeed political—dimension to Krishn's line of reasoning. He pointed to the reputational costs that Arjun would incur were he to

disregard his duty as a warrior and as an upholder of truth
and refuse to fight:

अकीर्तिं चापि भूतानि कथयिष्यन्ति तेऽव्ययाम् ।
सम्भावितस्य चाकीर्तिर्मरणादतिरिच्यते ॥

(Akeertim chaapi bhootani kathayishyanti teavyayaam
Sambhavitasya chaakeertim maranaadatirichyate.)

*People will always speak of the dishonour you would
incur (by not fighting)
And dishonour, for a respectable person, is worse
than death.*

—Bhagavad Gita, 2.34

Arjun was thus urged to not get entangled in the ways
of material attachment; instead, making himself equally
resistant to the vagaries of happiness and grief, he should
fight the good fight. He owed this to the universal good
that he stood for, and to himself as an individual.

Lessons for the every day

Irrespective of whether one's mettle is tested in an actual
war, the trials and tribulations that each and every one
of us faces every day are not to be underestimated.
Sometimes we get to choose our battles; more often than
not, though, we can find ourselves thrown into a fray of
petty politics amongst big egos and have to decide whether
to fight or not. The Bhagavad Gita offers some valuable
advice, but its message is alas too easily subject to crude

distortions. We address an important genre of these types of misrepresentations before unpacking the lessons of the text for our lives today.

A few years ago, one of the authors of this book gave a talk on the Mahabharat and India in Hamburg, Germany. Immediately after the talk, she was approached by an elderly German lady in the audience who conveyed (roughly) the following message to her, 'The Bhagavad Gita is a book of evil because it preaches violence. It favours fighting crusades.' She further suggested, 'If Krishn were really godly, surely he should have stopped Arjun from fighting the war.' Sadly, the German lady, for all her good intentions, had completely misunderstood the Bhagavad Gita. Perhaps her discomfort with the text derived from her de-contextualized reading of the text, as well as a pacifist sugar-coating of the German past that sometimes results in a condemnation (by some) of war under all circumstances.

Undoubtedly, a core message of Krishn to Arjun is 'Therefore, arise, son of Kunti, and fight!' (तस्मादुत्तिष्ठ कौन्तेय युद्धाय कृतनिश्चयः, Tasmatuttishtha Kaunteya yuddhaaya kritanishchayaha, Bhagavad Gita, 2.37). But this message was a product of a long and demanding context, throughout which the Pandavs had shown extreme tolerance to the wanton cruelty and spite of the Kauravs.[3] Despite the fact that Arjun and his brothers frequently turned the other cheek and exercised much self-restraint, childhood rivalries between the two sides transformed into deadly competition, which included attempts by the Kauravs to assassinate their cousins. Dodging such attempts and ignoring some vicious provocations, the Pandav brothers still managed to convert the barren share of land that Dhritarashtr had given them into a rich and prosperous kingdom; unable to see their kin flourishing, the jealous Kauravs then deprived them of their hard-won and rightful gains through a game of loaded dice. The game that took place in the royal assembly is regarded as the most disgraceful amongst the many heinous acts committed by the Kaurav brothers, in which the righteous Pandavs and their noble wife were publicly humiliated. Even though all in the royal court knew that the Kauravs had rigged the game, the Pandavs accepted—and duly fulfilled—the harsh conditions imposed on them as forfeit. They spent twelve years in exile, and the thirteenth incognito, before returning to Hastinapur to reclaim their part of the kingdom. The Kauravs denied them this and even refused to give them a symbolic set of five villages to govern. Duryodhan announced: 'No land shall I surrender to the Pandavs, not even that which can be pierced by the point of a needle.' When Krishn came to suggest treaty negotiations, the Kauravs tried to imprison him.

The reckless wickedness that the Kaurav side had come to embody—in the face of the kindly forbearance of the Pandavs and after multiple attempts to find a peaceful solution had failed—finally led to war. This war was one of *adharm* (untruth/transgression/evil) versus dharm (righteousness/duty/good), but it was not a jingoistic crusade of conversion.

Studied against this background and in its brief but deep entirety, the Bhagavad Gita offers us at least three important lessons for our daily battles.

First, war is never to be taken lightly or casually. It is a strategy of the last resort, and to be employed only after genuine attempts to find alternative solutions have failed. When faced with disagreements at the workplace, for instance, the 'war' equivalent would be to put in an official complaint to the Human Resources department. Such a step, however, will have little credibility if no attempt has been made to approach the other party beforehand, at least to inform them of the grievance and ideally also to find an amicable, bilateral solution to the conflict. Simpler, less costly and sustainable solutions can be lost if one is hasty in declaring war.

Second, to exercise caution against war does not translate into a fear of going to war, when necessary. For many Indians, amongst the most familiar lines from the Bhagavad Gita are the following:

कर्मण्येवाधिकारस्ते मा फलेषु कदाचन ।
मा कर्मफलहेतुर्भूर्मा ते सङ्गोऽस्त्वकर्मणि ॥

(Karmanyevaadhikaaraste maa phaleshu kadaachana
Maa karmaphalaheturbhoormaa te
sangoastvakarmani.)

*You are entitled to your action, but not the fruits of
your action.
Neither make rewards the motivation for your action,
nor become attached to inaction.*

—Bhagavad Gita, 2.47

And while firmly adhering to the notion *nishkaam dharm* (which roughly translates to selfless duty) that is captured by the above shlok, we are taught by Krishn that going to war can be one's duty. In certain situations, acceptance, fatalism, inaction are all the very opposite of fulfilling one's duty—such passivity must be firmly avoided. Neither should a war be launched solely for the sake of action, nor should it be conducted for the sake of narrow, selfish gains. Rather, the pathway to war is chosen in the defence of justice and truth. Applied to the every day, this means standing up for the right thing. This should be obvious enough when it involves the defence of another— for instance, the torment that is inflicted on animals in the name of human nutrition or tradition—and in such cases, it is our duty to offer sanctuary to animals in need, report animal abuse to the authorities and create awareness (and condemnation) of such cruelties via social networks. But sometimes, we as individuals can be subject to injustice too—as Arjun himself was, along with his brothers and wife, at the hands of the Kaurav princes. Insofar as the Bhagavad Gita argues for the oneness of the individual with the divine, there is no differentiation between standing up for others or oneself—what matters is that we do all we can to protect and defend the universal good.[4] And one should be willing to do this alone, if necessary.[5] For instance, if a worthy colleague (or oneself) is repeatedly bypassed for a promotion at work in favour of less qualified (but white/male/nepotistically favoured) candidates, a stand must be taken. 'War' here can include a range of options for the individual concerned, from appealing the case to leaving the institution for a more welcoming and appreciative terrain.

The third powerful takeaway is that once the path to war is chosen (and after all other measures have failed), there can and should be no turning back. While other chapters in this book highlight the importance the Mahabharat attaches to strategic flexibility, war requires commitment, persistence and even a degree of strategic lock-in. Reversal should be contemplated only if the other side produces the required behavioural change, or if one's own strategic position is unfortunately and debilitatingly weakened. This includes 'wars' that one might have to fight with one's own bad habits (such as poor nutrition) or to improve one's performance at a sport or in educational efforts, when an all-out commitment is needed. Arjun's last-minute qualms on the battlefield, while understandable, are not to be emulated: once involved in any effort on a war footing, there is no room for dithering.

Lessons for foreign policy and governance

Outside—and especially Western—perceptions of India and its people have tended to cluster at the two extreme ends of a clichéd, colonial spectrum. On the one hand are paternalistic, idealized stereotypes of an other-worldly people, entrapped in 'Hindu fatalism', and thus unwilling or unable to act in a determined and consequent way. On the other hand are ludicrous misrepresentations that try to paint India's growing self-confidence as militarism and fascism.[6] Perhaps a swing to the latter misperception is an almost inevitable consequence of the former. Having twisted and misunderstood India's tolerance as indicative of 'Hindoo' resignation and defeatism in the first place (and used such distortions as a reference point for centuries), external observers are likely to misinterpret the slightest assertiveness by India—historically or in the present—in a negative light as it goes against their original expectations. These tropes are problematic in their own right but also have real-world consequences that include repeated failures in diplomacy when dealing with India. A contextualized reading of the Bhagavad Gita may be a useful antidote for outsiders who wish to negotiate more effectively and constructively with India. India is neither gung-ho about taking on confrontations, nor is it afraid to take a clear and tough position (even in the face of considerable external opposition) when needed. We have seen this multiple times: in the aftermath of the nuclear tests of 1998, on the issue of the purchase of Russian oil in the aftermath of the Russian invasion of Ukraine, as well as on the question of access to vaccines and other pandemic-related treatments in World Trade Organization (WTO) negotiations. Had there been more awareness of India's deep-rooted negotiation traditions, Western diplomats would have better understood these positions and may have also been able to contribute to mutually supportive and constructive solutions.

The lessons of the Bhagavad Gita are also normatively relevant for foreign policy strategy at large. They apply not only to conditions that demand a full-blown war but also to other situations of potential conflict and confrontation. We share three such insights.

First, the war in which Arjun finds himself is the result of a series of failed negotiations. While the previous section highlighted the importance of treating conflict as a measure of last resort in our daily lives, this lesson is even more important in matters of high politics. A lock-in for war or hard bargaining should come in only when all other measures have failed. But the avoidance of war is not a goal in itself. Sometimes, deadlocks can only be broken by banging heads together, and an oppressive peace needs to be challenged through confrontation. Especially when core interests and values are at stake, some tough and consequent positions have to be taken.

An obvious example of this is the failure of the *Wandel durch Handel* strategy—change through trade—in attempting to engage with and socialize Russia and China into the liberal order. These attempts were made in good faith by not only the West but also the international community at large. They involved closer bilateral economic ties, membership of international organizations (such as the WTO: China acceded in 2001 while Russia in 2012) and status recognition via entry into old clubs (e.g. the transformation of the G7 into the G8 with the inclusion of Russia from 1998 to 2014) and new groupings (e.g. the creation of the BRICS—Brazil, Russia, India, China and subsequently South Africa, illustrating the camaraderie and cooperation amongst the rising powers of the Global South). However, as the growing assertiveness and expansionism of these authoritarian states have become apparent, the need to adopt tougher lines with both is now necessary for Western powers as well as democracies in their vicinity. This does not mean full-scale war. But it does mean taking tougher measures to reduce economic dependence (especially in strategically important sectors) and reconfiguring supply chains towards like-minded partners.

Second, neutrality is not an option. Krishn's message to Arjun is very clear: he must fight for the good, and this involves choosing sides when faced with an enemy that perpetrates cruelty, deceit and malice. There is no ambiguity that the Kauravs—despite some of the admirable traits of their heroes—have chosen the pathway of adharm or evil.

Some will baulk at this seemingly Manichean view of good versus evil, and instead emphasize the importance of the grey zones that require more nuance and create more scope for fence-sitting. Such indeed is arguably a position that India's foreign minister, S. Jaishankar, has used. For instance, in an agenda-setting speech in 2019, he spoke in favour of 'multi-alignment', 'India First' and 'hedging' as part of a 'strong and pragmatic policy outlook'. He argued, 'Hedging is a delicate exercise, whether it is the non-alignment and strategic autonomy of earlier periods, or multiple engagements of the future . . . The answer is in a willingness to look beyond dogma and enter the real world of convergences. Think of it, not just as arithmetic but as calculus.'[7] On another occasion, he remarked rather pithily, 'I think we should choose a side, and that's our side.'[8] This elegant framing may have worked well for India in the past and may also have had some appeal for other players amidst the euphoria of the post-Cold War era that promised technocratic solutions to multiple problems. But Jaishankar's logic has less traction in a world of polarization and growing imbalance.

A major power like India cannot afford to sit in the grey zone of neutrality when its own borders are threatened by a neighbour that does not share its values of democracy. The same applies to countries in Europe: witness the difficulties that Germany has had in disentangling itself from its over-dependence on Russia for energy supplies. Contra the argument made by Jaishankar and more in line with the lessons of the Bhagavad Gita, to choose one's own side sometimes requires a clear stance *against* an opponent and *in favour of* like-minded friends. Had the current or previous German chancellors, Olaf Scholz and Angela Merkel, respectively, read the Bhagavad Gita, their China strategy may have been clearer, more consequent and more effective. Rather than make a trip to China in November 2022 (and even worse, accompanied by a business delegation), Scholz could have served his own country, Europe and the democratic world by going to India instead. He could have used such a trip to offer closer economic and defence ties with the world's largest democracy (and thereby also facilitated a diversification of India's economic and defence sectors away from China and Russia, respectively).

There are times in our personal lives and in international politics when we must take a firm and principled stance. The Bhagavad Gita shows us when, why and how.

8

On Fake News and Disinformation: Dronaacharya, Yudhishthir and Ashwatthama

अनृतं जीवितस्यार्थे वदन्न स्पृश्यतेऽनृतैः ॥

(Anritam jeevitasyaarthe vadanna sprishyateanritaihi.)

He who utters falsity to save a life is not touched by (the sin of) speaking a lie.

—Mahabharat, VII.190.47

Dronaacharya was the greatest of teachers. A Brahmin (i.e. belonging to a priestly family) by birth but afflicted by poverty, he had ended up choosing the Kshatriya (warrior's) way of life. The Kaurav and Pandav cousins owed their remarkable martial skills to the training that they had received under his devoted guidance. Dronaacharya was loyal to Bhishm and Dhritarashtr: at a time when he and his family had suffered through penury and humiliation, the Kauravs had given him employment and respect. Hence, even though he shared a special bond with the Pandavs, and especially his favourite student Arjun, Dronaacharya remained on the side of the Kauravs during the great war. Upon Bhishm's fatal injury on the tenth day of the war, Dronaacharya was appointed commander-in-chief of the Kaurav army.

Under attack from Dronaacharya—the master of strategy, a fighter of immense skill and ferocity, and commander of many celestial weapons—the Pandavs found themselves beset with heavy losses. Their teacher was proving impossible to vanquish, immune to the strategies that the Pandav heroes employed and the weapons they wielded.

नैष युद्धे न संग्रामे जेतुं शक्यः कथंचन ।
सधनुर्धन्विनां श्रेष्ठो देवैरपि सवासवैः ॥

(Naisha yuddhe na sangraame jetum shakyaha
kathamchana
Sadhanurdhanvinaam shreshtho devairaipi
savaasavaihi.)

In neither war nor battle, can he be defeated
Armed with his bow, even amongst the gods and
inhabitants of the earth, he is the best archer.

—Mahabharat, VII. 190.10

Dronaacharya was unstoppable. Observing the rapid decimation that their army was going through, Krishn advised the brothers that they must destroy Dronaacharya's spirit to demobilize him.

Dronaacharya had only one weakness: his beloved son, Ashwatthama. It was for the sake of Ashwatthama—to enable the family to enjoy a life together of honour and comfort—that Dronaacharya had given up his preferred path of being a sage and instead embraced the identity of the warrior-teacher. Ashwatthama had grown up with the royal princes, and his fealty for the Kaurav side ran deep (perhaps even deeper than his father's as it was entwined with a genuine friendship with Duryodhan). Trained by his father and having had the brave Kaurav and Pandav brothers as classmates to spar with, he had turned out to be a formidable and valiant warrior in his own right. The deep love that Dronaacharya bore his son was public knowledge. Krishn advised the Pandavs to exploit this weakness and came up with a villainous plan: Dronaacharya should be told that his son had been killed in battle. This false news would cause their renowned guru such intolerable grief that he would lay down his arms in despair. The Pandavs could then gain an advantage in the war.

The immorality of this plan was obvious to all. But the Pandav brothers agreed to it, deeming this to be the only way. The strongest of the Pandavs and wielder of the mace, Bheem, then struck a terrible blow to a gigantic elephant, killing him. This majestic elephant had fought on the side of the Pandavs, bravely inflicting severe damage on the Kaurav side, but had the misfortune of also being called Ashwatthama. Having thus killed a namesake of Dronaacharya's son, the Pandavs could now truthfully claim: 'Ashwatthama is dead.' Dronaacharya's son was to be kept embroiled in another corner of the battle so that the claim of his death could not be verified.

On hearing Bheem's announcement that Ashwatthama had been killed, Dronaacharya was shaken to the core. But rationality soon replaced his immediate emotion: Ashwatthama had outstanding proficiency with weapons and was almost impossible to thwart on the battlefield. Surely this news could not be true. And reassuring himself thus, Dronaacharya leapt back into the battle with renewed force.

Seeing that Dronaacharya was less gullible than initially assumed, Krishn recognized that the false news would have to be conveyed by a source of the highest credibility. Yudhishthir, the son of Dharm and renowned for always speaking the truth, was such a source; were he to announce the news of Ashwatthama's death, Dronaacharya would have no other choice but to believe the fake news.

To bring Yudhisthir on board, Krishn first pointed out
that unless Dronaacharya were stopped, the entire Pandav
army would not survive beyond half a day. Urgent action
was needed. And second, he stated:

अनृतं जीवितस्यार्थे वदन्न स्पृश्यतेऽनृतैः ।

(Anritam Jeevitasyaarthe vadanna sprishyateanritaihi.)

He who utters falsity to save a life is not touched by
(the sin of) speaking a lie.

—Mahabharat, VII.190.47

Yudhishthir complied with the plan, while still attempting
a compromise that he felt he could live with. In the
interest of victory for the Pandav side, he confirmed
to Dronaacharya that Ashwatthama had been killed.
Still loath to tell an outright lie though, he muttered
under his breath 'Ashwatthama the elephant'. These
qualifying words were rendered deliberately inaudible to
Dronaacharya, and the central falsehood—Ashwatthama
has been killed—produced the intended, brutal effect.
Broken, Dronaacharya laid down his weapons and
withdrew into a *samadhi* (a stage of intense meditation
that enlightened individuals could assume before death).
Drishtadyumn—the commander of the Pandav army,
whose life's purpose was to kill Dronaacharya[1]—seized
the opportunity. Ignoring Arjun's pleas that his (unarmed,
grief-struck and immersed in a final meditation) teacher

be left alone in peace, the son of Drupad and brother of Draupadi mercilessly beheaded Dronaacharya.

The treacherous killing of Dronaacharya secured the Pandavs a strategic advantage that they needed. The damage to the Kaurav side was immense. But the act of lying also produced deep, moral scars on the Pandavs. Yudhishthir's chariot had, until this incident, floated four inches above the ground—a testimony to the purity of his heart that always spoke the truth. With the lie uttered by one who should have known better, Yudhishthir's chariot sank to the ground, symbolizing his fall from grace.

Lessons for the every day

There is much that is distressing and ignominious in this story: the killing of an elephant who had only loyally served on the side of his killers; the fatal exploitation of a father's love for his son; the ruthless killing of one unarmed. But we chose this ancient story not to shed light on human turpitude; rather, it appears in this collection for an unfortunate but interesting resonance that it has for the present on the subject of 'fake news'.

Dronaacharya was the victim of what we would today call a politically motivated disinformation campaign. The Pandav strategy had the classic characteristics of disinformation. The 'news' of Ashwatthama's death was deliberately manipulated with the killing of Ashwatthama the elephant. Pronouncements of 'Ashwatthama is dead' were intentionally made out of context. To legitimize the fake news, a highly credible channel of communication—Yudhisthir, the personification of truth and goodness—

was chosen. Verification was rendered impossible by ensuring that Dronaacharya's son was kept preoccupied in another, distant part of the battle. The lie was created and disseminated with a targeted purpose: to demoralize—and in effect paralyse—a warrior who was indispensable for the enemy side.

Three counterfactuals around this episode are interesting, all of which would have allowed the continuation of Dronaacharya at the helm of the Kaurav army and transformed the course of the war. To start with, had Dronaacharya been more guarded in revealing his closeness to his son, the Pandavs would not have been able to exploit his weakness in the first place. Second, had there been better ways to keep the different fields of the battle connected, the spuriousness of the claim of his son's death would have become evident with a quick fact-check. Third, had he not believed the usually trustworthy Yudhishthir, Dronaacharya would have been able to battle on until his son's return—and then invest renewed energy into the battle. Unable to withstand his onslaught, the Pandav army would have been decimated in half a day, exactly as Krishn had predicted. The war would have ended with a victory for the Kauravs.

Unfortunately for the Kauravs, Dronaacharya's circumstances did not afford him these counterfactual luxuries. First, to hide any indication of his love for his son would have required decades of secrecy, bordering on the level of paranoia. Recall, after all, that the Pandavs too—like the Kauravs—had been his students from a very young age; a relationship of mutual trust was only natural amongst them. Covering up such a key aspect of his identity as a devoted father, and that too amongst friends on a permanent basis, would not have been an easy task for Dronaacharya; indeed, it would have been tantamount to living a lie. Second, the battle of Kurukshetr took place in the BC era; bar a boon of divine sight that was endowed to Sanjay (which allowed him to narrate all the events of the war to the blind king, Dhritarashtr), this was not an age of instantaneous or even swift communication. Communication channels amongst the different (and fraught) battlefields to connect Ashwatthama and Dronaacharya, which would have enabled verification of the false news, did not exist. Combine the above two points, and we get to the third: it was almost inevitable that Dronaacharya would believe a piece of tragic news that not only Bheem, but even the noble and dependable Yudhishthir—both his own, trusted pupils—were conveying to him.

While Dronaacharya was thus unable to defend himself against fake news, we have a wider range of options available to us. Three takeaways follow for individuals living in a global society today, where misinformation and disinformation are rife.

First, one should be more tight-fisted in sharing personal data and private details. This is especially so in a world of increasing digitization, where hacks, fine print and differentiated laws across jurisdictions on data privacy and data sharing can leave us more vulnerable than ever to the misuse of revealed (sometimes inadvertently revealed) information.

Second, while Dronaacharya did not have access to modern technology to verify the fake news of his son's death in a faraway battle, we do have the means to do so. We owe it to ourselves and to others that we do not internalize or disseminate information without verifying it.

This includes checking the trustworthiness of the source, cross-checking across diverse credible sources, nipping false narratives in the bud (when possible), and reporting cyberattacks and potential fakes. This may not be easy amidst the time pressures for immediate reactions, which social media and news cycles have come to demand. But with the privilege of being able to exercise our voice (that modern-day digital technologies facilitate) comes a responsibility of constant vigilance.

Third, learning from Dronaancharya's understandable but ill-fated willingness to believe a normally reliable Yudhishthir, we would be well served to exercise a healthy dose of scepticism towards all sources. Even the best news channels can sometimes get the facts wrong; policymakers can rely on narrow discipline-specific expertise at the expense of other relevant considerations; scholars of the ivory towers too can be driven by perverse incentives.[2] These ambiguities leave considerable room for manipulation, for those inclined to misuse the media–academia–policy interfaces. The only way we can overcome this as individuals is to read and collect data widely, and by constantly challenging existing assumptions and trends.

Besides the safeguards that individuals can put into place themselves, good governance institutions and foreign policies also have an important role to play in preventing or reducing the adverse effects of disinformation, as discussed in the next section.

Lessons for foreign policy and international politics

Disinformation campaigns can operate at several levels with severe political consequences. While this story shows us that using strategies of disinformation goes back to ancient times, digital technologies provide a much wider arena and opportunity for their ready use. We highlight three takeaways for foreign policy and global governance below.

First, narratives matter.[3] The narrative of 'Ashwatthama is dead' had devastating consequences for Dronaacharya. Neither its veracity nor whispered qualifications to it ('Ashwatthama the elephant') mattered; what mattered was it was being conveyed by sources to whom the targeted recipient attached trust and credibility. And narratives are even more consequential today, given their ability to go viral via digital routes and have an amplified impact upon the physical world.

The power of narratives unfortunately is sometimes more readily grasped by authoritarian states. Recall, for instance, the Nazi motto, 'If you tell a lie big enough and keep repeating it, people will eventually come to believe it,'[4] or the use of troll factories by Russia that seek to spread support for the war against Ukraine on social media.[5] In contrast, liberal-democratic institutions find themselves hamstrung on this front for ethical reasons. Additionally, upholders of liberal democracy often suffer from a complacency about their own hold over 'The Truth', which they also assume should be obvious to all other enlightened people (and if this is not obvious, then the people are clearly yet to see the light—so goes the implicit and convoluted logic). International organizations (such as the WTO, International Monetary Fund, World Bank and the United Nations) epitomize this proclivity: having long tended to assume that the 'facts' and numbers/ statistics speak for themselves, they usually make scarce effort to draw even on competing disciplinary insights (let alone meaningfully engage with the wider public at large).[6] To have a serious chance at winning wars, maintaining peace or bringing about reform, political and international leaders will be well-served to remind themselves of the power of narratives.

Second, recall that Dronaacharya lacked the technical means to verify the veracity of the news of his son's death in a timely way. The digital sphere affords us far greater opportunities to cross-check facts in real time, but it also presents us with a whole new set of challenges. More effective governance of this terrain is necessary.

In the absence of a cohesive set of global rules to regulate the misuse of digital technologies, we see a wide range of their adverse effects at work. These include political interference in democratic processes and fundamental disruption to essential infrastructure (by states as well as rogue actors). The threats emanate from 'Big Tech' (a few US-based companies that 'possess the ability to harness the digital gold rush—along with the equally overwhelming influence on discourse in democratic societies') as well as 'Red Tech' (coming from China, which, 'with its rapid successes in building a vibrant technology ecosystem, has unleashed plans to dominate innovation, high technology and the global perceptions ecosystem').[7] Both threats are expanding globally: the former, for instance, via commercially viable social networking platforms; the latter via sale of surveillance technologies and infrastructure to other states (and especially in the Global South).

To deal with these threats, more effective coordination amongst democracies is needed. On the issue of regulating the internet, India has often found itself on the side of

China and others pushing against a free and open internet, and instead emphasizing the importance of sovereignty.[8] But there are other ways and other potential partners. The EU, having led the way on data privacy via its General Data Protection Regulation, could be a useful ally for India: together, these two major markets would be able to set new and ethical standards, and discover new friends in the process.

Third, the unexpected resort to deceit by the normally honest Yudhishthir offers a tough reminder that trust should not be easily bestowed under conditions of conflict. And if even old friends and former pupils could turn against their guru, it was hardly surprising that Drishtadyumn—born with enmity in his heart against Dronaacharya—readily embraced his role as Dronaacharya's assassin. In the context of the modern day, this is a cautionary tale against relying on rival states (and their state-owned enterprises) for communication technologies and vital infrastructure. For instance, rather than accept investment from China in ports or 5G, European countries would be better served by building up their own alternatives—in collaboration with other suppliers and markets (including India, Japan and the US).

Knowing the tools and methods of disinformation can help us build strong defences against them. Dronaacharya's sorry experience shows us how we might avoid falling prey to such tactics.

9

On the Importance of Flexibility and Adaptability: Karn and the Snake-Prince

न नाग कर्णोऽद्य रणे परस्य बलं समास्थाय जयं बुभूषेत् ।
न संदध्यां द्विव शरं चैव नाग यद्यर्जुनानां शतमेव हन्याम् ॥

(Na naag Karnoadya rane parasya balam samasthaaya
jayam bubhooshet.
Na sanddhyaam dviva sharam chaiva naag
yadyarjunaanaam shatameva hanyaam.)

*Oh Snake, Karn does not wish to claim victory on the
strength of another.
I would not mount the same arrow twice, even if I
could kill a hundred Arjuns.*

—Mahabharat, VIII.90.47–48

It was the seventeenth day of the war, and the battlefield of Kurukshetr was awash with blood. The Kaurav side had suffered grievous losses. The Pandav brothers and their legions had incapacitated some of the most experienced and skilled of the Kaurav generals. Bhishm lay fatally wounded on a bed of arrows, awaiting his chosen hour of death. With his heart broken by the fake news of his son's death, Dronaacharya had laid down his weapons and had been killed subsequently by Drishtadyumn. Brave Karn had stepped in as the Kaurav commander-in-chief on the sixteenth day of the war.

It had always been clear that Arjun and Karn would meet as adversaries, one day. Both were sons of Kunti and supremely skilled archers; both also bore a long-standing rivalry against each other, which had transformed into a bitter animosity over the decades. Just before the outbreak of war, Kunti had revealed to Karn that he was, in fact, her first-born child, whom she had abandoned at birth. She had then entreated him to join the Pandav side and fight together with his brothers against the Kaurav princes. Karn, loyal to a fault, had refused to abandon Duryodhan but had made Kunti a promise: he would target only Arjun, and spare the other brothers, so Kunti would still have five sons when the war was over—with either Arjun or Karn himself slain in battle.

As expected, the combat between Arjun and Karn was one of great ferocity. Arrows rained across both sides and covered the skies. It was becoming apparent, however, that Arjun was getting the better of Karn. Hearing the fray, a snake emerged from his underground abode. His name was Ashwasen and he was a prince of snakes—a *nagraj*. Ashwasen's special powers included the ability to fly and assume a terrifying form whenever he so wished. This noble snake bore a sworn enmity to Arjun. Many years ago, the Pandav brothers had—in order to build their capital of Indraprasth (modern-day Delhi)—razed the thick and luscious Khandav forest to the ground. At the insistence of Agni, the god of fire, they had sealed the forest as it burnt, thereby making escape impossible for its many and diverse, innocent, more-than-human[1] inhabitants. Ashwasen's mother had been killed in the carnage, even as she had tried to protect her son; Ashwasen was one of the very few survivors. When he saw the combat taking place between Karn and Arjun, he believed that the time to avenge his mother's death had finally come.

Ashwasen climbed into Karn's carriage and then into his quiver of arrows. In this quiver was a special arrow, which Karn had worshipped with much care and nurtured with devotion, bearing one, sole purpose in mind: Arjun's destruction. Recognizing the need for the use of a powerful weapon against Arjun (whose arrows were inflicting severe pain and damage on his foe), Karn now drew on this arrow. Unbeknown to Karn, Ashwasen the snake-prince had placed himself on this arrow. With Karn's penance and the snake-prince's intrinsic powers (plus his quest for justice for his mother's murder), this arrow was now virtually invincible. Karn took aim. Although Ashwasen was invisible to all human eyes (including Karn's), the god Indr (of the thousand eyes) saw the magnificent creature that had reinforced the arrow, and trembled at the impending death of his son, Arjun.

Observing this highly potent arrow about to strike, Lord Krishn—as Arjun's charioteer—asked his beautiful, white horses to kneel to the ground, and he further lowered the chariot with his foot. The chariot sank. Karn's charioteer, Shalya, warned that the arrow would miss its target; Karn should reconsider and realign his aim.

What followed is described in the verse below:

अथाब्रवीत क्रोधसंरक्तनेत्रो मद्राधिपं सूतपुत्रस्तरस्वी ।
न संधत्ते द्वि:शरं शल्य कर्णो न मादृशा जिह्मयुद्धा भवन्ति ॥

(Athaabraveet Krodhasamraktanetro madraadhipam
sootaputrastarasvi.
Na sandhatte dvihisharam shalya karno na maadrashaa
jinhayuddhaa bhavanti.)

*The swift son of a charioteer (Karn), his eyes red with
anger, responded.*
*Karn does not shoot the same arrow twice, brave
warriors like me do not engage in such devious
practices.*

—Mahabharat, VIII.90.26

Refusing to reconsider his aim, Karn shot his prized arrow, and—as predicted by Shalya—missed. The precious and powerful arrow knocked off Arjun's radiant crown, but it did not injure its bearer in the slightest.

Ashwasen slid out from the arrow and returned to Karn's chariot, now assuming his formidable and glorious form. He offered that he would once again mount Karn's arrow; were Karn to make use of this reinforced arrow and release it after taking all aspects into consideration, the death of Arjun—their common foe—would be certain. On being asked by Karn, he also revealed his motivation for supporting Karn. Working together as allies, they would now surely be able to defeat Arjun.

Karn refused the offer to join forces with Ashwasen. He responded: 'Oh Nag, Karn does not wish to claim victory on the strength of anyone else's support. Besides, I would not shoot the same arrow twice, even if it were to slay one hundred Arjuns.'

Hurt and disappointed to find his mutually beneficial offer thus rebuffed, Ashwasen decided to launch an attack on Arjun alone, unaided. Krishn immediately warned Arjun that the flying serpent headed towards them was a dangerous adversary. Arjun took aim, fired without hesitation and his precise arrow pierced through the body of the snake-prince.

Thus died the brave Ashwasen, in the battle of Kurukshetr. But the story did not pan out well for Karn either. In a few hours, our tragic hero too would meet his death. What could have been a win-win game for both Karn and Ashwasen had unfortunately been transformed into one where both incurred fatal losses and ended up empowering their joint enemy.

Lessons for the every day

Amongst the many turning points in the battle, this story—albeit not amongst the most well-known from the Mahabharat—represents an important one. Karn's peculiar sense of honour and stubbornness not only cost him his own life but also resulted in the death of Ashwasen (a fellow-creature who had already suffered dearly at the hands of Arjun via the brutal burning of the Khandav forest and the killing of his mother). Had Karn realigned his aim as per Shalya's advice, his precious arrow would not have missed its mark; had he accepted the second chance that Ashwasen had offered him, he might still have been successful in vanquishing Arjun; had Arjun indeed been vanquished, the tide could still have turned in favour of the Kaurav army as late as the seventeenth day of the war. Instead, the war ended the next day and was still followed by many brutalities and further deaths.

This counterfactual thought experiment is not to make a normative case for a Kaurav victory; rather, its purpose is to demonstrate how fatally injudicious Karn's approach turned out to be for himself, the unfortunate snake-prince, as well as Karn's own friends, comrades and people whom he had fought so hard to protect. Two main takeaways follow.

First, even though Karn stands out in the Mahabharat for his generosity and loyalty,[2] just as striking is his lack of flexibility, which stems in good measure from his difficult origins.[3] Karn's stubbornness and a misguided sense of pride prove to be his undoing in the battle with Arjun; even after being warned that he will miss, he refuses to realign his arrow and thereby ends up using his especially designed and cherished weapon in vain. In real life, while it is important to stand by one's principles, emulating Karn's obstinacy will also likely turn out to be a losing strategy. The saying, 'Being holier than the Pope' sometimes springs to mind when one reads about Karn, and perhaps we all sometimes need guarding against this type of an error. The ability to adapt—according to the problem one faces, one's own altered circumstances, one's interlocutors and an ever-changing context—is a vital attribute to win in any real or metaphorical battle, however large or small, and indeed also to winning friends and influencing people in non-confrontational settings. Krishn, in contrast to Karn, is the epitome of adaptability and flexibility, standing firm on principled choices with regard to the end goal of dharm, but still pragmatically using, whenever needed, a variety of (sometimes dubious) means to achieve those goals.[4]

Second, Karn seems to be reluctant to learn from prior mistakes. Despite having seriously scuppered his chances through his headstrong refusal to realign his arrow, he was offered a second opportunity by Ashwasen. Opportunity knocking twice is rare, and yet, Karn did not seize it. He did not acknowledge his erroneous aim that had lost him his prized arrow. If anything, he was even more insistent that he would stick to his principles, thereby replacing the *ends* with the *means* themselves as the primary goal. Hence, for instance, with the same arrogance that he had shown Shalya, Karn now told Ashwasen that he would not fire the same arrow twice (even if this would allow him to kill a hundred Arjuns). In fact, this would not have been the same arrow at all; it would have been another arrow, which the snake-prince would have reinforced with his strength and skill. Karn, however, seemed to regard it as the same arrow, perhaps because it involved being supported by the snake-prince, and thus taking the same form of a Nagaastra as the previous weapon. By lacking the humility that is essential to update one's strategies and behaviour patterns, Karn seems to have doomed himself to repeating the same mistakes—eventually with disastrous consequences.

Lessons for politics and foreign policy

Just as important are the lessons that this story offers on questions of governance and foreign policy. We now flag up two: on alliances and strategic flexibility.

First and foremost, Ashwasen came to the aid of Karn when he was losing the fight; an ally of the snake-prince's determination and strength could have been exactly what the Kaurav side needed. Undoubtedly, one should be wary of Trojans bearing gifts. But Ashwasen was no Trojan; he had already revealed his history of enmity with Arjun. This could have turned out to be not just an alliance of convenience but a partnership based on deeply held concerns (thereby addressing questions of both interests and values). And yet, Karn refused to accept this hand of friendship. Through his misplaced sense of pride and rigidity of strategy, Karn squandered away a potentially vital asset.

In terms of foreign policy of the present day, this suggests a need to move away from the approach that the Indian foreign minister, Jaishankar, and indeed some of his predecessors have adopted. When asked about whose side India is on, Jaishankar has stated, 'I think we should choose a side, and that's our side.'[5] This 'Ent-like' philosophy gets a lot of applause in India.[6] But it is not one that we would recommend: sometimes, to choose one's own side, it is important to join forces with others via formal and informal alliances. This may be especially relevant amidst times of severe imbalances of power, as is currently the case with China's authoritarian advance in Asia and globally. Going it alone, as Karn tried to do—or indeed hedging[7]—might not be a good idea when faced with a Great Power neighbour and adversary, with a history and philosophy of expansionism.

The second foreign policy takeaway is on the importance of maintaining flexibility in one's strategic choices; facts change, and smart policymakers are able to change their minds and policies accordingly. Karn illustrates the great harm he caused himself, his side and Ashwasen, first by refusing to realign his arrow despite Shalya's advice, and then again by refusing to fire an arrow supported by Ashwasen. Instead, he stuck to his principle of neither realigning his aim nor shooting the same arrow twice. What was needed, in contrast, was strategic flexibility: to update in response to new information and to learn from past mistakes, and thereby adapt his strategic choices.

Apply this to the modern day and we have no dearth of examples to work with. For instance, in the 2000s, attachment to the BRICS may have made more sense for India; for India to now still find itself in China's corner, be this over the Russian invasion of Ukraine or trade and development issues in the WTO, is unfortunate, to say the least. As the fact of Chinese predominance changes, India needs to adapt its old strategies, balance against China, and work more proactively with new friends including the US, EU, NATO and others. India's participation in the Quad is an interesting but small step in the right direction.

We can offer an even more resounding critique on missing strategic flexibility with respect to other players. Germany and the EU's China strategies are 'how-not-to'[8] examples of this. The Russian invasion of Ukraine should have driven home the risks of over-reliance on authoritarian states, particularly regarding key supplies of energy or strategically important products. The trip by the German chancellor Olaf Scholz accompanied by a business delegation in 2022, with little coordination with the EU or even Germany's key partner France, showed little indication of any learning regarding this. A belief in the 'socialization' of authoritarian states via increasing economic exchange may have been justified in the early 2000s;[9] today, however, a major update in strategy is needed, which recognizes the risks of the weaponization of interdependence.

The story of Karn and Ashwasen gives us illustrations of two different types of issues that affect the foreign policy considerations of many countries: on the one hand, the need to look for—and serve as—a reliable ally, and on the other hand, to show strategic flexibility in response to changing imperatives. These may seem to be contradictory. In reality, they are not, when grounded in the pursuit of core meta-values, such as dharm.[10]

10

On Compassion and Ecologism: The Story of the Noble Parrot and the Tree

अनुक्रोशो हि साधूनां महद्धर्मस्य लक्षणं ।
अनुक्रोशश्च साधूनां सदा प्रीतिं प्रयच्छति ॥

(Anukrosho hi sadhunaam mahaddharmasya
lakshanam
Anukroshashch sadhunaam sadaa preetim
prayachchati.)

*Compassion is the characteristic of the greatest dharm
of pious souls.
The compassion of the pious always bestows love.*

—Mahabharat, XIII.5.24

The great war was over, the Pandav brothers had won, and Bhishm lay wounded on a bed of arrows, awaiting his chosen hour of death.

In preparation for kingship, Yudhishthir sought the wisdom of the great grandsire and wished to learn about the duties of a good king, rule of law, social order and the nature of good conduct. Despite his extreme pain, Bhishm answered his questions with patience and care. In Bhishm's precepts are contained some from the most beautiful, even if lesser-known, stories from the Mahabharat. The story in this chapter is a particular favourite for all three of us.

Yudhishthir requested Bhishm, 'I would like to learn about the characteristics of kind and devoted people.' Bhishm answered, 'The ancient dialogue between Indr—the king of gods—and the magnanimous parrot is a powerful illustration of this,' and went on to narrate the following story.

The hunter, the tree, the parrot and Indr

A greedy hunter, eager for his kill, shot a poisoned arrow towards a deer. The lethal missile missed its mark. Instead, it pierced the heart of an old, gigantic, resplendent tree that was the sanctuary of many birds and animals. The poison was fierce, and it spread through every vein of the tree. The leaves of the tree withered, its fruits fell, its bark started peeling off. It was clear that the tree was dying. Seeing that the shelter and succour of their home was rapidly depleting, all the residents of the tree left for stronger branches and greener pastures—all creatures but one.

In the hollow of the tree lived a parrot. This noble bird refused to abandon the dying tree. And as the tree withered away, so did the parrot, grieving with the tree. Soon, without access to fruit or seeds, the bird became weaker and weaker, and was no longer able to sing or talk as he had usually done. Unlike fair-weather friends, the parrot—with unusual fortitude and endurance—showed constancy and loyalty to the tree in tragic times.

The king of the heavens and the gods, Indr, observed this unusual bond between the parrot and the dying tree. He could not quite believe that a bird could show so much empathy. He decided to investigate the matter. Assuming the guise of a Brahmin (priest), Indr descended on earth, and asked the parrot, 'Oh noble bird, why do you not abandon this tree?'

The bird bowed his head respectfully and answered: 'Oh, king of gods, I welcome you. My years of penance have allowed me to see through your disguise.' Indr was now even more impressed and decided to test the parrot: 'This tree is now bereft of leaves and fruits. It is no longer fit to offer shelter to birds. You have an entire forest before you, with beautiful trees laden with fruit, rich with safe hollows and lush with leaves—why do you resist these offerings and instead choose to serve this sorry stump of a tree? This tree has reached the end of its lifespan, it has no more strength, its soul is destroyed, its beauty is gone. Is it not time for you to now do the intelligent thing and abandon this old tree?'

Upon hearing Indr speak thus, the pious parrot responded with humility: 'This tree was my home when I was born. It was here that I learned many virtues. This tree treated me as if I were its own child. It kept me safe and protected me from many foes. For these reasons, I bear great love and devotion to this tree. Compassion to this tree is my dharm. When this tree was strong and capable, it gave me refuge; how can I possibly abandon it when it is now helpless and weak? Please do not waste your efforts in trying to persuade me to forsake this tree—for forsake it I cannot and will not.'

अनुक्रोशो हि साधूनां महद्धर्मस्य लक्षणं ।
अनुक्रोशश्च साधूनां सदा प्रीतिं प्रयच्छति ॥

(Anukrosho hi sadhunaam mahaddharmasya
lakshanam
Anukroshashch sadhunaam sadaa preetim
prayachchhati.)

Compassion is the characteristic of the greatest Dharm
of pious souls,
The compassion of the pious always bestows love.

—Mahabharat, XIII.5.24

Hearing these gentle and moving words of the parrot filled Indr with joy. He offered to grant him a boon. The generous-hearted parrot did not ask for anything for himself. Instead, he asked the king of gods to restore the tree to its former splendour of green glory.

Indr was now even more moved by the parrot's unshakeable devotion and noble character. He immediately sprinkled the tree with the nectar of immortality, Amrit. The tree came to full bloom again, with majestic branches, leaves and fruit. The parrot continued to reside in the secure arms of his beloved tree for the rest of his long life and found a welcoming abode in Indr's heavenly kingdom for the forever after.

Bhishm concluded this story by emphasizing the following moral: *through the compassionate companionship of a devoted ally, one can attain all desires.*

Lessons for the every day

This story is especially relevant amidst the insufferable damage that humans are inflicting on all other species across the planet. For resources, for food, in the name of cultural practices and sometimes for crass entertainment[1] trees are felled, forests destroyed, animals murdered and entire ecosystems devastated. We do this even when the going is good; crisis times produce still worse exploitation of the planet. The parrot, however, behaved very differently from most of our fellow humans, even in the face of an existential threat.

The parrot showed admirable compassion and loyalty for the dying tree. Even though he could not save the tree on his own, he still thought it worthwhile to remain with it, sharing its suffering and pain. The primary driver for the bird's behaviour was his elevated sense of dharm or morality (as the text also suggests several times), and at considerable jeopardy to his own life. Importantly, though, the rewards of his altruism were not reserved solely for the afterlife: both the tree and the parrot received ample recompense with a joyous and long life shared together, as a boon from Indr. And while the story itself emphasizes the sacrifices that the parrot was willing to make for the tree, we should not forget (just as the parrot did not) the love and shelter with which the tree had effectively raised the parrot. Their love was mutual, and their trans-species friendship eternal.

Four vital takeaways follow for our daily lives.

First, one should not forget the kindness received from others. The debts that we owe to our diverse supporters and well-wishers in life are many. These debts should be honoured, and the devotion and trust that a friend bestows on one should be reciprocated wholeheartedly.

Second, these debts are not restricted to human friends. The parrot reminds us of a kinship that transcends species. He likened the tree to a protective parent and reciprocated its care with devotion and love. If we came even a few steps closer to this ideal and learnt to think about other species as our kin, we could reduce the brutal and gratuitous mistreatment of animals and protect ourselves at the same time. Such protections include avoiding the emergence of new and deadly viruses that result from zoonotic jumping, preserving biodiversity and balance in the environment, and mitigating climate change. Trans-species compassion creates vital win-win situations, which our dominant anthropocentric narratives have thus far led us to ignore.

Third, compassion begins first and foremost at home, for all the pets and strays that grace our lives. In a sense, the parrot and the tree were a microcosm of an ecosystem. This kindness, however, need not be restricted to the local level. Nature at large deserves the same respect. In a globalized and interconnected world, we can all do our part in fighting cruelty against animals and the destruction of forests: be this the war on street dogs in Turkey (or indeed, the horrific attacks on stray dogs in Kerala, which led #StopKeralaKillings to trend on Twitter), the live animal markets of China, trophy hunting in Africa or the destruction of wildlife habitats across a range of countries.

And finally, the parrot was the very antithesis of the throwaway culture that modernity has taught itself as a habit. Instead of wrecking different environments and moving on (with talk now rampant of colonizing other planets), we would be well-served by treating what we already have with respect and affection.

Lessons for politics and foreign policy

In the magic and mythology of the Mahabharat, animals can sometimes talk. The parrot was thus able to speak on behalf of the tree and convince Indr to restore the tree to life. But who speaks on behalf of the voiceless in the real world? The story of the parrot and the tree asks us to rethink our priors on whose voices and interests are represented in domestic politics and foreign policy. Across our different professions—*karmabhoomi*—we can make a difference on this matter.

Some non-governmental organizations have been fighting for the rights of animals. For instance, Sandra, an orangutan held in a zoo in Buenos Aires, became the first ape to be granted the same rights to life, liberty and freedom from harm as her human captors.[2] But most animals are not so fortunate. We see a key research task for both political scientists and legal philosophers to investigate how the interests of diverse animals can be integrated into a fairer political system. This should matter, especially if one is committed to true and inclusive democracy in the broadest sense.

The story of the parrot and his beloved tree further prompts a rethinking on narratives about climate change, sustainability and biodiversity. All three issues, in one way or another, involve 'saving the planet'. Interestingly, however, most dominant narratives on these topics remain human-focused. The 'Fridays for Future' movement is a case in point, in which children and young adults seek to mobilize action to deal with the climate emergency. Just how anthropocentric these narratives are is illustrated in the speeches of Greta Thunberg, who pioneered these protests. Addressing world leaders at the United Nations Climate Action Summit 2019, Thunberg declaimed: 'You have stolen my dreams and my childhood with your empty words . . . You are failing us. But the young people are starting to understand your betrayal. The eyes of all future generations are upon you, and if you choose to fail us, I say, we will never forgive you.'[3] Although Thunberg is right to alert the world to her disappointment regarding the inadequacy of climate action, her narrative is narrow and self-entitled.

Thunberg and others see the dangers of climate warming in terms of their own futures as well as children in other parts of the world; at best and at its least selfish, the case that is made in much Western scholarship is about *intergenerational* justice. This entire movement for climate action seems to be premised on the assumption that the planet belongs to humans; there is almost no recognition that animals, plants and a multitude of other creatures might also have some claim to it. Sustainability questions resemble this anthropocentrism, with a view to human consumption in mind rather than the well-being of fish and other living 'resources'. Biodiversity considerations at least recognize the harm that destruction of multiple species causes in terms of systemic balance but seldom consider the suffering and pain endured by individual animals that leads to the endangerment/extinction of a species. Even Green Party politics in Europe,[4] rather disappointingly, suffers from similar limitations of anthropocentrism.

Primarily gender-focused policy debates across countries today fail to take into account obvious trade-offs involved, including the allocation/reallocation of scarce resources. Generous parental policies and subsidies/allowances for children (as is the case in northern Europe, and seen as models for many other countries to aspire to), for instance, may achieve feminist goals but come at the cost of eco-friendly goals that require limiting further encroachments on planetary space and resources. Taken against discussions about whether India can really sustain its growth and development goals given its huge and growing population, it is hard not to see the gendered politics and policies in rich countries as being tinged with elements of racism. If we take into account the lessons offered by this (and other) stories from the Mahabharat, it is clear that public policy in rich and poor countries needs to balance considerations of economic growth and gender politics on the one hand with ecological preservation and trans-species justice on the other.

In the realm of foreign policy, recent attempts across different countries to develop a 'feminist foreign policy' appear to us as rather unambitious for the reasons outlined above.[5] Foreign policies, especially of democratic states, should be doing everything possible to protect nature and the environment. This involves changing multilateral rules (for instance on trade) to allow for preferential treatment of countries that have more 'humane' policies towards animals (towards pets, urban animals, farmed animals and wildlife). It requires widening the concept of 'human' rights that are not restricted to humans only[6]—an idea that occurs in several stories from the Mahabharat. India too, as the home of these ideas that date back to ancient times, should be playing a proactive role in setting this agenda. For far too long, swathes of politicians (not only Indian) have repeated 'वसुधैव कुटुम्बकम्' (vasudhaiva kutumbakam; the entire earth is one family) almost to the point that it has become a platitude.[7] It is high time that India reminds its own people as well as its international interlocutors that this concept of the 'earth' and 'family' includes all species, and backs its talk with actions to protect animal lives (including a major updating of the Prevention of Cruelty to Animals Act, 1960).

Using a more mundane, anthropocentric lens too, the story of the parrot and the tree underlines the importance of inclusion and friendship in public policy and foreign policy, respectively.

The parrot refused to 'other' the ailing tree; instead, he chose to remain inseparable from the tree that had sheltered him since childhood, thereby binding their fates together. Governments, in their attempts to deal with Covid-19, have shown considerable variation in their 'othering' narratives (especially towards the elderly and the vulnerable), sometimes with devastating consequences.[8] Even as governments, increasingly across the world, are removing all Covid-19 restrictions and declaring the pandemic over, the costs of such policies are highlighted poignantly in an open letter by journalist Jeanine Santucci:

> The sad truth is that our country's politicians decided to prioritize their elections and popularity over our health. I choose to listen to science, epidemiology and immunology experts over politicians refusing to acknowledge that COVID-19 is airborne and that masking and clean air are the most effective tools we have.
>
> The other main reason I am still taking this seriously, and I hope you will, is that our country's most vulnerable people deserve to be part of society. With the removal of mask mandates in health care settings and essential places such as pharmacies, public transit and grocery stores, immunocompromised people are made outcasts. Telling disabled and chronically ill people to 'stay home forever' is cruel.[9]

Santucci is referring specifically to the policies of the US, but her message applies easily to most governments in both the Global North and the Global South. Even as infections rise, the virus mutates and avoidable deaths occur, governments can still choose a better way, as illustrated by the parrot's identification of its own interests with those of the tree's. Governments *can* institutionalize norms and rules for a new normal. Measures towards this would include a continued insistence on social distancing, requiring testing, prioritizing ventilation, and assuring flexible formats for study and work that always enable hybrid options. Facilitating this new normal would signal that the government values *all* its people, and not just the strong and the young. It is likely that such measures will prove not just to be altruistic; as numerous medical professionals report the increasing incidence of life-threatening (and fatal) Covid-19-triggered conditions and ailments across all age groups,[10] showing caution now may turn out to be to the benefit of not 'just' the old and the weak but also to those who have believed themselves to be immune to the worst effects of the virus.

Russia's loyalty to India on the issue of Kashmir offers us a powerful example in foreign policy matters that time-tested friendships produce valuable pay-offs. This commitment dates back to December 1955, when Nikita Khrushchev, the first secretary of the Communist Party of the Soviet Union, and Nikolai Bulganin, the Premier, visited Jammu and Kashmir. At a time when there was a strong push to internationalize the problem from the West as well as China and force India to conduct a plebiscite under UN supervision, the Soviet Union firmly backed India's position that this was to be treated as a bilateral issue. It did so not only in words but in deeds, over the decades, and despite changes in its own leaderships and borders, consistently blocking every Security Council Resolution that sought UN intervention over Kashmir. It further came to India's assistance during the 1965 and 1971 wars with Pakistan. Much is now made of India's excessive dependence on Russia for its military supplies, which has no doubt contributed to the country's reserve in condemning the

Russian invasion of Ukraine or backing Western sanctions against Russia. But use the lens provided by the story of the Mahabharat, and neither India's habitual readiness to rely on Russia—a time-tested friend—for its military needs nor its current reluctance to join in games of Russia-bashing is surprising.

If the West wants to make use of the altered geo-strategic context (where there should be serious concern amongst all democracies, including India, about the growing dependence of a weakened Russia on China, and the deepening bonds between these two authoritarian powers), a good start will be to show itself to be a *reliable* friend. The shenanigans of the US and the EU in Afghanistan did not signal such reliability nor do the continued attempts by major European players to woo China for business. Lord Palmerston may have said that Britain had no eternal allies and no perpetual enemies; 'our interests are eternal and perpetual, and those interests it is our duty to follow'[11] India, however, shows that the situation is more complex and more interesting than that. Interests can get bound up with the fates of friends, and memories of old friendships die hard. Trust and compassion matter, perhaps more than ever amidst the churning imbalance of power across the globe.

11

On Animal Rights and Personhood: Yudhishthir and the Dog

भीतं भक्तं नान्यदस्तीति चार्तं
प्राप्तं क्षीणं रक्षणे प्राणलिप्सुम् ।
प्राणत्यागादप्यहं नैव मोक्तुं
यतेयं वै नित्यमेतद् व्रतं मे ॥

(Bheetam bhaktam naanyadasteeiti chaartam
Praptam ksheenam rakshane praanalipsum
Praanatyaagaadapyaham naiva moktum
Yateyam vai nityametad vratam me.)

One who is afraid, has shown devotion, has no one else to turn to,
Has sought refuge with me, or is incapable of protecting himself,
I will not abandon such a being even upon death,
Such is my eternal vow.

—Mahabharat, XVII.3.12

After a long and peaceful reign, the Pandav brothers and Draupadi embarked on their final journey towards salvation: *mahaprasthaan.*

Retiring from the kingdom, the royals made their way to the Himalayas. They would have to renounce their celestial weapons on the way and would be unaccompanied by their entourage. The journey itself was long and was expected to be fraught with hardship and pain. The rules that governed the process were strict. If any of the exhausted fellow-travellers were to fall to their deaths, it was imperative that the rest of the party continue in the effort to reach heaven, without looking back. Even as they departed on this gloomy and last expedition, a stray dog began to follow them and became a part of the group.

One by one, the brave Pandavs succumbed to their deaths. Draupadi was the first to fall, followed by Sahadev, Nakul, Arjun and Bheem. Each one of them bitterly asked why they had failed to attain heaven. With a heavy heart, Yudhishthir answered that their respective sins and frailties had resulted in this consequence. Draupadi, for all her virtues, had been partial to Arjun and had not treated all the brothers equally. Sahadev,

Nakul and Arjun had all fallen for the sins of vanity and arrogance: Sahadev had been excessively proud of his intelligence, Nakul of his handsome looks, and Arjun of his skills as an archer and warrior. Bheem's sins were gluttony and boastfulness. Finally, Yudhishthir found himself to be the only surviving Pandav, together with the dog still by his side.

As the dog and the eldest Pandav continued on their climb, the skies and the earth suddenly echoed with a joyous fanfare, announcing the arrival of Indr. The king of the gods himself had come, driving his chariot, to invite Yudhishthir to ride up to the heavens with him.

Yudhishthir requested Indr to allow his dead brothers and wife to accompany him, for he had no wish to enter heaven without them. Indr reassured him that the Pandavs had already left their mortal bodies and reached heaven; Yudhishthir need have no fear for he would be reunited with his beloved family.

The eldest Pandav then addressed Indr again: 'Oh lord of past and present, this dog has been constantly faithful to me, please permit him to accompany me; I do not have any cruelty within me (and to leave him behind would be an act of ruthless brutality).'

Indr responded: 'You have been bestowed with immortality, you are being made an equal with me, you are being granted immense riches and unprecedented spiritual attainment; seize the joys of heaven now and leave this dog behind—there is no cruelty in doing so.'

Yudhishthir stood firm. He respectfully addressed Indr again: 'Oh god of a thousand eyes, for a moral person, it is especially difficult to engage in lowly conduct; I hope I am never united with worldly riches or spiritual joys, which accrue by abandoning one who is devoted to me.'

The argument continued. Yudhishthir reiterated his position:

भीतं भक्तं नान्यदस्तीति चार्तं
प्राप्तं क्षीणं रक्षणे प्राणलिप्सुम् ।
प्राणत्यागादप्यहं नैव मोक्तुं
यतेयं वै नित्यमेतद् व्रतं मे ॥

(Bheetam bhaktam naanyadasteeiti chaartam
Praptam ksheenam rakshane praanalipsum
Praanatyaagaadapyaham naiva moktum
Yateyam vai nityametad vratam me.)

*One who is afraid, has shown devotion, has no one else
to turn to,
Has sought refuge with me, or is incapable of
protecting himself,
I will not abandon such a being even upon death,
Such is my eternal vow.*

—Mahabharat, XVII.3.12

Indr refused to be swayed by Yudhishthir's argument. He tried a different tack. He reminded Yudhishthir that dogs were considered to be inauspicious creatures. Religious sacrifices and charitable acts would be rendered fruitless should a dog's gaze fall upon them. Only by abandoning this dog would Yudhishthir be able to achieve heaven, advised Indr. Besides, Yudhishthir had forsaken his

brothers and wife with far less hesitation; why was he so
enamoured by this dog?

To these arguments too, Yudhishthir's answers were
calm and clear. 'One thing is certain: there can be neither
friendship with nor opposition to the dead. It was not
possible for me to bring my brothers and wife to life. It
was only when they had died that I decided to leave them
behind.' And he further posited:

भीतिप्रदानं शरणागतस्य स्त्रिया वधो ब्राह्मणस्वापहारः।
मित्रद्रोहस्तानि चत्वारि शक्र भक्तत्यागश्चैव समो मतो मे ॥

(Bheetipradaanam sharanaagatasya striyaa vadho
brahmansvaapahaaraha
Mitradrohastaani chatvaari shakra
bhaktatyaagashchaiva samo mato me.)

To abuse/frighten anyone who has sought refuge with
one, to kill a woman or a religious/spiritual person,
To betray a friend—for me, these four sinful acts
in aggregate are morally as despicable as the one
heinous act of abandoning one who has been devoted
and faithful.

—Mahabharat, XVII.3.16

At this point, the dog transformed to reveal his true,
divine identity. He was Dharm—the god of righteousness,
truth, time and death—and also Yudhishthir's birth
father. Yudhishthir had now passed the final test. The
god thus spoke:

अभिजातोऽसि राजेंद्र पितुर्वृत्तेन मेधया।
अनुक्रोशेन चानेन सर्वभूतेषु भारत ॥
अयं श्वा भक्त इत्येवं त्यक्तो देवरथस्त्वया ।
तस्मात् स्वर्गे न ते तुल्यः कश्चिदस्ति नराधिपः ॥

(Abhijaatoasi rajendra pituvritten medhayaa
Anukroshen chaanen sarvabhooteshu Bhaarata.
Ayam shvaa bhakta ityevam tyakto devarathastvayaa
Tasmaat swarge na te tulyaha kashchidasti
naraadhipaha.)

Through your virtue, intelligence and compassion
towards all creatures,
You have truly proven yourself to be the worthy son of
your father
(. . . I had tested you earlier too as the yaksh of
the lake . . .)
This time too, by insisting, 'This dog is faithful to me,'
you were willing to renounce Indr's chariot
For this reason, heaven has no king equal to you.

—Mahabharat, XVII.3.18, 21

Yudhishthir then ascended to heaven, accompanied
by the gods and other celestial beings, celebrating his
goodness. He was also given a unique honour amongst
all mortals—he alone was allowed to enter heaven with
his physical form intact. By standing true to his loyal,
canine friend, Yudhishthir had attained salvation and
enlightenment.

Lessons for the every day

Animals in a variety of settings—as pets, as street animals, in zoos, in farms and in the wild—are subject, by human hand, to immense misery. This ranges from gross neglect and abandonment to unspeakable cruelties and outright torture. Yudhishthir's refusal to abandon the dog, in the face of multiple temptations—offered by the king of gods himself—is a much-needed reminder to humans, in times that have become especially difficult for our 'more-than-human' friends. For this, he received the ultimate reward—a place with the gods. For us, Yudhishthir's loyalty to his faithful companion offers three sets of lessons: on useful ways to act, on defying traditions that entail cruelty, and on challenging prevalent norms to facilitate mindset shifts.

Through our actions

Through a few, simple acts, we can imbibe the lessons of this story in our daily lives. At a minimum, the story requires us to take full responsibility for our pets (and not abandon them when the economic going gets tough, or when caring for them interferes with our lifestyles, or when the pets grow older and lose their novelty value). And whether we are pet-owners or not, we can all do a great deal to prevent the pervasive cruelty to animals that we see around us.

In India and Turkey, this cruelty has been visible recently on the streets in the gratuitous violence that is being meted out to stray dogs. In China, it can be seen in the horrific conditions of live animal markets as well as large-scale farming practices. We still see pictures of trophy hunting in parts of Africa. In the West, these brutalities enter our homes via the meat and milk industry. Even though these terrible practices may sometimes seem overwhelming and impossible to fight, each one of us can make a difference via our own actions and via the voices that we exercise in our social circles and social media. Stray dogs deserve protection and adoption—not beatings and worse. Products with 'exotic' animal parts can and should be boycotted, and cruelty against animals should be called out—within our own societies or with reference to the nations we trade with. Trophy hunting—or indeed hunting as a sport—deserves social condemnation; the killing of animals as a show of power or 'for fun' must be recognized as being beyond the realm of acceptability. And each and every one of us can make changes to our lifestyles to embrace more vegetarianism and veganism.

By challenging traditional wisdom

Bringing about such change is not easy, sometimes even for oneself or one's inner circle, let alone society at large. It may be essential to challenge existing norms, some of which rest on centuries of tradition or survive in the name of religious practices. Here again, Yudhishthir offers us an inspiring example. Even when the king of the gods himself appeals to religious beliefs in making the case against the dog and urging him to abandon the animal, Yudhishthir stands firmly by his canine companion: trans-species compassion and loyalty trump religious precepts and even divine advice. Sometimes, protecting animals will require taking a stance against established thinking and societal beliefs that are justified in the name of religious convictions and ancient traditions (akin to the pushback that women's rights encountered across different societies). At times like these, remembering Yudhishthir's actions can help strengthen our own resolve.

Yudhishthir rejects not only arguments made purportedly in favour of his interests (the gain of heaven, which he is willing to forgo rather than leave the dog behind) but also values (as the son of Dharm and known to be the most virtuous of the noble Pandavs, he is expected to behave in line with religious prescriptions). He stands by his canine friend, even when it means going against the king of the gods himself. He knows that the consequence of taking this position may turn out to be that he will no longer be allowed his hard-earned place in heaven. The son of Dharm—the very personification of duty through much of the Mahabharat—is turning out to be quite the iconoclast. But in fact, read Yudhishthir's comebacks to Indr, and we see that he goes even further: he offers a fundamentally non-anthropocentric world view that underpins his arguments.

Through his answers to Indr, Yudhishthir is indirectly attributing *personhood* to animals, which is indistinguishable from the personhood that is attributed to humans. At no point does he accept Indr's argumentation that the dog is lesser than a *human* person. Despite being robustly questioned, taunted and pressured by Indr, he keeps repeating, 'this dog is devoted to me'. In his own argumentation, when he lists those worthy of protection, he makes no distinction between animals and humans. The human–animal divide is prominent in its absence in Yudhishthir's verses: for Dharmaraj Yudhishthir, there is no distinction across species, no hierarchy and no primacy for humans. Indeed, in Yudhishthir's eyes, animals deserve not only kindness and compassion (which could have been an easier and still credible case to make) but also the same respect and dignity that most will accord only to (some) fellow humans.

In taking this approach, Yudhishthir is living up to a powerful ideal advanced by the Bhagavad Gita:

समं सर्वेषु भूतेषु तिष्ठन्तं परमेश्वरम् ।
विनश्यत्स्वविनश्यन्तं यः पश्यति स पश्यति ॥

(Samam sarveshu bhooteshu tishtantam
parameshwaram
Vinashyatsvavinashyantam yaha pashyati sa pashyati.)

He who sees the divine in all creatures,
And in all mortal bodies sees the immortal soul, he is
the one who truly understands.

—Bhagavad Gita, 13.28

By challenging prevailing norms

The inspiring ideal that Yudhishthir provides us with is notably different from one that pervades many conversations today, especially in the West.

Note, for instance, the discussion in the previous chapter on the underlying anthropocentrism of Fridays For Future protests across Europe. Greta Thunberg's language of 'You have stolen my dreams and childhood' has been embraced by well-meaning children and their parents alike; as a result, across different walks of life, people are making the case for saving the planet for their children and grandchildren. While the goal of 'saving the planet' is a most worthy one, the reasoning for it is inadequate, if we apply Yudhishthir's wisdom to the problem. Yes, the planet deserves to be saved, but not only for future generations of humans; it needs to be protected for the sake of the many species (and individuals) of animals, fish, plants and other beings who are equally rightful inhabitants of this planet.

In India too, recent years have seen the appearance of an ancient phrase in common parlance: 'वसुधैव कुटुम्बकम्'(*vasudhaiva kutambakam*). Most people who repeat this phrase, however, translate it as 'the world is a family', and do so with reference to relations amongst *people* or states. In fact, this verse means a lot more than that.

The Sanskrit verse from which this phrase is derived is:

अयं निजः परो वेति गणना लघु चेतसाम् ।
उदारचरितानां तु वसुधैव कुटुम्बकम् ॥

(Ayam nijaha paro veti gananaa laghu chetasaam
Udaaracharitaanaam tu vasudhaiva kutumbakam.)

This is mine, this is yours—only mean-minded people
indulge in such counting,
For the generous-minded, the entire earth is one family.

—Mahopnishad, 6.71[1]

The term 'vasudha' refers to the 'earth' and the verse does not mean that the community of man is one family; rather it refers to *all beings*—human and more-than-human—of this planet as one family. Rather than be reduced to a glib and anthropocentric catchphrase, this is a motto of trans-species inclusiveness that deserves to be carefully reflected on, internalized and lived.[2]

Compassion and dignity that transcends species is morally important, first and foremost because such an approach can reduce needless suffering of sentient beings. This should be incentive enough for all of us to follow Yudhishthir's example. Additionally—for more selfish reasons—it results in gains in the shape of immeasurable love, loyalty and devotion from adopted and rescued animals. Most humans who have shared their homes with stray and abandoned dogs will vouch for the fact that the return on their small investment is usually priceless. And all that besides, there are reasons of (self and public) interest at its most basic—survival—for humans to show more respect towards animals. For instance, zoonotic spillover—caused due to the severe maltreatment of animals by humans—is a major cause for pandemics. The paragraph below, which appeared in an op-ed in the *New York Times*, summarizes the issue perfectly:

> ... harming animals can lead to considerable harm to humans. This provides a self-interested reason—in addition to the even stronger moral reasons—for humans to treat animals better. The problem is that even self-interest is an imperfect motivator. For all the puffery in calling ourselves Homo sapiens, the '*wise* human,' we display remarkably little wisdom, even of a prudential kind.[3]

Yudhishthir had it right. There is a lot we can do to learn from this story at the individual level. But what does this mean for the purposes of global governance, foreign policy and matters of high politics?

Lessons for foreign policy and global governance

Amidst growing concerns about climate change, some attention has been paid to issues of sustainability and biodiversity. Unfortunately though, even with the best intentions, the narrative remains primarily anthropocentric.

The conservation agenda is a case in point. Conservation is defined as 'the act of protecting Earth's natural resources *for current and future generations*'. A distinction is drawn between conservation and preservation: the former refers to sustainable use of nature by humans, whereas the latter involves 'protecting nature from human use'. Even the goal of 'preservation', however, is framed in terms of prevention of 'mass extinction' of various species.[4] Little thought is given to the gross indignities, pain and brutal deaths suffered by Cecil the lion, Freya the walrus and the hundreds of thousands of nameless animals who continue to experience unimaginable human-induced indignities and violence on a daily basis.

A part of the problem lies in the fact that the scholarship on more-than-human 'personhood', albeit rich, has remained rather a niche affair, concentrated in the sub-fields of philosophy, anthropology and law. Experts in the more applied fields of political science (e.g. security studies and political economy) are only recently beginning to venture into this difficult terrain. Within political science too, questions of voice and representation are usually premised on notions of rationality, rather than sentience; this, in turn, narrows the scope for building more inclusive polities and societies. Further, as the foundations of research today have been built mainly on Western intellectual traditions, 'more-than-human' voices (that we do 'hear' in the Mahabharat and other Indian texts, for instance, but also across other cultures[5]) are unrepresented in research, politics and policy.

Were scholars of international relations even cursorily familiar with the story of Yudhishthir and the dog (and indeed several others that occur in the epic, including the story provided in the previous chapter), they might be more willing to break down the binaries between 'human' and 'non-human'. Then, what we might get is more openness to recognize that many sentient beings have the cognitive capacities that are associated with personhood (and are deserving of both social and legal recognition as 'persons').[6] The real-world impact of this could be significant, given especially that fields such as public policy and international relations are usually closer to the worlds of policy and practice, in comparison to other fields that are further ahead in developing a consensus on this (e.g. on the issue of phenomenal consciousness) but do not operate so closely at the academic-policy interface.

Bring in more engagement with such approaches from the Mahabharat and other 'liberal' traditions (that emphasize the rights of the individual—human or not—person, for instance) from the Global South, and a variety of narrative and policy shifts could follow. Animal welfare would move from the fringe to the mainstream. Tougher laws would be enacted that severely punish crimes against animals.[7] Domestic subsidy programmes would have to change to promote vegetarianism and veganism. Social policies that support the growth of human populations would have to be balanced by ecologically oriented policies. Trade agreements would reflect the prioritization of the goal of animal rights; countries with records of maltreatment of animals would stand to lose most-favoured-nation (MFN) privileges. 'Value-based' diplomacy could be infused with real meaning and consequence. And trade-offs between human development and protection of more-than-human lives could finally be reconciled by building a new, genuinely inclusive model of globalization that ensures the dignity, security and well-being of all lives.

Acknowledgements

This book brings together our collective knowledge, hopes and strivings. The act of writing it together has been an extraordinary honour and privilege.

We owe a great debt of gratitude to our families for having encouraged us to embark on this adventure.

Aruna Narlikar and Amrita Narlikar are indebted to two very special humans: Dr Vanamala Bhawalkar and Professor Anant Narlikar. Vanamala, a pioneering scholar on the Mahabharat, led the way for her daughter, Aruna, and grandchild, Amrita, to develop a love for this subject. Anant—Aruna's husband and Amrita's father—is a master storyteller. He brought to life many of the stories we present here, and we cannot thank him enough for the lively debates we had at the dining table, his constant encouragement and his readiness to help in every possible way. Aruna and Amrita also acknowledge the joyous presence and reliable support of the family's four-legged member—Don: family jester, devoted protector and wise soul. Also known as the #VeryGoodBoy in some circles, his gentle kindness and intelligence further opened us up to a more non-anthropocentric perspective that several stories from the Mahabharat entail. We take this opportunity to also thank the many other beings who have graced our lives: Lakshmi the elephant; Caesar, Monty, Coco, Snoopy a.k.a. Batasha, Roshani—the hounds; and the many animal- and bird-friends we have made across continents.

Amitabh Mattoo grew up with his grandmother, *Didaji*, Krishna Kumari Mattoo, introducing his brother and him to the Mahabharat as bedtime stories, and to Ramdhari Singh Dinkar's epic poem in Hindi, *Rashmirathi*, on the life of Karn. Neerja Mattoo, his mother, encouraged a love for reading from an early age, including of the great Indian epics. Amitabh's wife, Ajita Mattoo, brought home the twelve volumes of the *Shrimad Bhagwatam*, also known as Bhagwat Purana, one of the great Puranas of Hinduism, which includes a detailed account of the life of Lord Krishn. Ishita and Vandita, and their faith in their father's eclectic interests, were reason enough for Amitabh to work on this terrific project initiated by Aruna and Amrita.

Our decision to write this book came, in part, from within. The Mahabharat is a text that is close to our hearts: it is a key portion of the civilization that made us and connects us with thousands of souls over the centuries. As its insights continue to help us through good times and trying times alike, we thought it was important and useful to share the eternal wisdom of this great epic with others. Additionally, though, we were responding to external demand. Amrita and Aruna had already had a book published on India's negotiation culture and the Mahabharat (*Bargaining with a Rising India: Lessons from the Mahabharata*, Oxford: Oxford University Press, 2014). Both Aruna and Amrita are very grateful to Dominic Byatt and Desmond King at OUP for their support with a project that was rather unique at the time and also therefore somewhat risky. That the book continues to receive much appreciation from scholars and practitioners of international relations, negotiation and foreign policy is, for us, a vindication of the trust that Dominic and Des placed in us. The enthusiastic response to this book also convinced Amrita and Aruna of the idea of doing a book that would share the insights of the Mahabharat with a wider readership. Aruna thus wrote short articles on the Mahabharat, which were published in the prestigious 'Speaking Tree' column of the national Indian broadsheet, *Times of India,* and was moved by the warm take-up and feedback from the readers. Amitabh had a similar experience when he applied lessons of the Mahabharat to foreign policy in an op-ed that he wrote for *The Hindu* and a journal article in *International Studies.* Amrita had been doing short, motivational videos on Twitter in Sanskrit-Hindi and Sanskrit-English combinations; these too generated much interest and enthusiasm, both from Indian viewers and globally. Our colleagues, friends and contacts on social media platforms addressed us with stimulating questions and asked us for more writings and multimedia engagement. We could not resist and thank all these diverse readers and audiences for their encouragement. We were especially delighted to take on this task when Milee Ashwarya offered us a contract with Penguin Random House and we thank her for her strong backing for the project at each step of the way.

This book is first and foremost the brainchild of Aruna Narlikar. In this team of authors, her connection with the epic and cognate texts is the closest. It was her idea to focus this book on the *stories* from the Mahabharat (more on this in the Introduction), and she is the one who has guided the team through the beautiful Sanskrit verses.

The contributions of Aruna's co-authors to this project came in addition to their 'day jobs' and amidst various other research endeavours. In this sense, this book does not derive immediately from the projects and grants that they have been awarded. Amrita and Amitabh can confirm, however, that the research they conducted as part of their projects has been directly relevant to this book; without the insights of their work in cognate areas, it would have been impossible for them to take on this task.

Amrita Narlikar is grateful to the following institutions for research funding: the Berlin-based SCRIPTS Cluster of Excellence for the projects *Leadership Types and Pandemic Narratives* and *Challenge to the Challenge: Responses to BRI from the Global South* (and for great conversations with Mark Hallerberg, Nora Kürzdörfer, Tanja Börzel and Michael Zürn); the Federal Ministry of Education and Research on the project *World Order Narratives of the Global South* (together with Ulrich Mücke, Eckart Woertz and Jürgen Zimmerer); and the Leibniz Association on *Transfer for Transformation* (where Amrita is principal investigator but works closely with her team to develop innovative forms of knowledge transfer, dissemination, access and impact). These projects are housed at the German Institute for Global and Area Studies (GIGA), where Amrita has served as President for almost a decade. She is grateful to her GIGA colleagues, Sonja Bartsch, Patrick Köllner, Peter Peetz, and especially to the wonderfully patient, strong and kind, Julia Kramer, for her cheery support on multiple fronts over many years. A research sabbatical allowed her an exemption from her teaching duties, and she thanks both the University of Hamburg and the Hamburg Ministry for Research and Education for ensuring this. She is also thankful to the other research institutions with which she is affiliated, and colleagues there who offer much collegiality and stimulating exchanges: Darwin College at the University of Cambridge, the Observer Research Foundation (ORF, Delhi), Research and Information System for Developing Countries (RIS, Delhi) and the Australia India Institute at the University of Melbourne.

Amitabh is grateful to three remarkable institutions and the community of scholars there who helped further his interests in thinking about Indian perspectives on international relations: the University of Oxford, Jawaharlal Nehru University (JNU) and the University of Melbourne. JNU is one of India's most formidable institutions in the humanities and social sciences and continues to provide a sanctuary to explore ideas and alternatives, however subversive they may seem, and challenge, as they often do, the orthodoxies of established wisdom. At Oxford, especially through the collections at the Indian Institute and the Bodelian, Amitabh accessed a new world of scholarship on the early texts of India. He taught about India and the world at the University of Melbourne and many of his ideas were shaped by the cutting-edge scholarship of students and scholars in the Faculty of Arts at the university. Amitabh was the founding CEO/director of the Australia India Institute, which generously provided support for much of the research work that he is currently engaged in, including a deep dive into the Mahabharat.

Numerous friends, well-wishers and colleagues supported us in different and invaluable ways. We are thankful to all of them. Heeraman Tiwari, *Guruji*, a friend and kindred spirit, helped Amitabh understand the nuances in the writings of his teacher, the Oxford philosopher Bimal Krishna Matilal, including the brilliant essay: 'Krsna: In Defence of a Devious Divinity'. For the interest and encouragement that they offered, Aruna and Amrita are especially grateful to Sachin Chaturvedi, Andreas Cichowicz, Markus Gehring, Gerhard Homuth, Simon Leadbeater, Vaibhav Purandhare, Samir Saran, Stephan Steinlein, Cecilia Sottilotta and Paul Tschöcke.

As explained in the Introduction, besides the pioneering Bhandarkar Institute's authoritative critical edition, we also used several other editions of the Mahabharat. We appreciate the different versions for different reasons. But the Bhandarkar Oriental Research Institute (BORI) deserves a special note of thanks for helping us with a reference that we were having difficulty in locating. Having an institution such as BORI to turn to is a great asset, and the entire team deserves to be commended for its important work.

Writing this book together was so invigorating that we must admit to a sentiment that we had never experienced with our other books: we were actually sad when we completed this one! This was not only because we achieved a new level of nerdiness by playing games involving this timeless epic. As we worked through the ancient stories, we found ourselves thinking in novel ways about modern problems. We also observed that we had begun to read parts of the Mahabharat in a new light as we applied its insights to problems of high politics and the every day. We got to square some circles and solve some dilemmas that had troubled us (which was most satisfying), and we found new problems to puzzle over (on which we plan to keep working). As we sign off this little book, we wish our readers their own memorable journeys through life, hopefully enriched with at least a few insights from the great Indian epic.

Notes

Chapter 1

1. Edward N. Lorenz, 'Predictability: Does the Flap of a Butterfly's Wings in Brazil Set off a Tornado in Texas?', American Association for the Advancement of Science, 139th Meeting, Massachusetts Institute of Technology, 29 December 1972, https://eapsweb.mit.edu/sites/default/files/Butterfly_1972.pdf (accessed 11 August 2023).
2. Tweet by Nicholas A. Christakis, 27 February 2020, https://twitter.com/nachristakis/status/1233065532947140610 (accessed 11 August 2023).
3. R.E.A. Almond, M. Grooten, D. Juffe Bignoli, and T. Petersen (eds), *Living Planet Report 2022: Building a Nature-Positive Society*, World Wildlife Fund, 2022, https://wwflpr.awsassets.panda.org/downloads/lpr_2022_full_report_1.pdf (accessed 11 August 2023).
4. Staple analyses of characters and dilemmas of the Mahabharat for us have been: V.S. Sukthankar,

On the Meaning of the Mahabharata, Monograph IV (Bombay: The Asiatic Society of Bombay, 1957); Bimal Krishna Matilal, 'Krsna: In Defence of a Devious Deity', in Jonardon Ganeri (ed.), *Ethics and Epics: The Collected Essays of Bimal Krishna Matilal,* Vol. 2 (Oxford: Oxford University Press, 2002); Vanamala Bhawalkar, *Woman in the Mahabharata* (Delhi: Sharada Publishing House, 1999).

5. We have deliberately chosen stories we think will be useful and inspirational for addressing modern-day problems. Our sampling should not create the mis-impression that we agree with all the different pieces of advice and injunctions that the Mahabharat offers. There are episodes and treatises in the Mahabharat which, in our perspective, cannot even be justified as being products of their own times, let alone as serving as exemplars for action today. And then there are contradictory recommendations in the epic (e.g. on the caste system, role of women, status of animals and environmentalism, among others)—inevitably so, given that the Mahabharat grew over the centuries via oral traditions across the country. We would argue that neither its heroes are to be idolized, nor its villains to be demonized; each episode needs to be read without resorting to moral relativism.

6. The Sanskrit verses that we cite in this book are referenced with the Gita Press edition; we provide our own translations.

7. S. Jaishankar, *The India Way: Strategies for an Uncertain World* (Delhi: HarperCollins, 2020); Amrita Narlikar and Aruna Narlikar, *Bargaining with a Rising India: Lessons from the Mahabharata* (Oxford: Oxford

University Press, 2014); Gurcharan Das, *The Difficulty of Being Good: On the Subtle Art of Dharma* (Delhi: Penguin Random House, 2010);C. Raja Mohan, 'The Mirror of the Epic', *The Bookshelf,* Institute of South Asian Studies, National University of Singapore, 006, 18 September 2020, https://www.isas.nus.edu.sg/wp-content/uploads/2020/09/BR-006.pdf (accessed 11 August 2023); originally published in *Indian Express,* 8 September 2020, https://indianexpress.com/article/opinion/columns/india-foreign-policy-china-border-row-ladakh-conflict-s-jaishankar-mea-6587070/ (accessed 11 August 2023); Amitabh Mattoo, 'Lessons from an Immortal Conversation: On the Deep Insights that the Mahabharata can offer', *The Hindu,* 19 February, 2021, http://www.amitabhmattoo.com/wp-content/uploads/2014/10/Lessons-from-an-immortal-conversation_- on-the-deep-insights-that-the-Mahabharata-can-offer-The-Hindu.pdf (accessed 11 August 2023).

8. For example, a recent piece by one of the authors of this book draws on several ancient Indian insights to argue that under India's presidency, the G20 has a unique opportunity to develop a fresh approach towards a kinder, fairer and more secure form of globalization, as well as a fundamental reform of the rules of global governance that underpin it; see Amrita Narlikar, 'Ancient Wisdom for Today and Tomorrow: India's Presidency of the G20', *Raisina Files 2023,* 2 March 2023, https://www.orfonline.org/expert-speak/ancient-wisdom-for-today-and-tomorrow/ (accessed 11 August 2023).

Chapter 2

1. For instance, the Bhagavad Gita, which forms a part of this colossal poem, begins with the following question by the blind king Dhritarashtr to his charioteer, Sanjay (who is gifted with divine vision that allows him to observe all that is happening in the battlefield):

धर्मक्षेत्रे कुरुक्षेत्रे समवेता युयुत्सवः ।
मामकाः पाण्डवाश्चैव किमकुर्वत सञ्जय ॥

(Dharmakshetre Kurukshetre samaveta yuyutsavaha Maamakaha Pandavaashchaiva kimakurvat Sanjay?)
Tell me Sanjay: gathered in the battleground of Kurukshetr—the battleground of dharm—eager to fight, what did my sons and the sons of Pandu do?
It is noteworthy that Dhritarashtr equates Kurukshetr with the battleground where the fight between dharm and adharm will be fought.

2. To be precise, five of the eighteen parts of the Mahabharat describe, in rich detail, all that transpires in and around this great war of the Bharat dynasty; other parts also contain reflections on the risks, benefits and consequences of war.

Chapter 3

1. Henry Farrell and Abraham Newman, 'Weaponized Interdependence: How Global Economic Networks Shape State Coercion', *International Security* 44: 1, 2019, pp. 42–79.

2. The post-war global trade order was underpinned by the most-favoured nation (MFN) status treatment: all contracting parties enjoyed the same market access

and other privileges. This system worked effectively for several decades and contributed to development and poverty reduction globally. However, under conditions of weaponized interdependence, a new system may need to be put in place that significantly relaxes the MFN presumption to facilitate deeper ties with select partners.

3. Christoph Hasselbach, 'Germany Woos India as an Ally against Russia', Deutsche Welle, 24 February 2023, https://www.dw.com/en/germany-woos-india-as-an-ally-against-russia/a-64811737 (accessed 11 August 2023).

4. 'EU and India Kick-Start Ambitious Trade Agenda', Directorate-General for Trade, European Commision, Brussels, 17 June 2022, https://policy.trade.ec.europa.eu/news/eu-and-india-kick-start-ambitious-trade-agenda-2022-06-17_en (accessed 11 August 2023).

5. Interestingly, Modi has connected the cause of environmental protection to the country's ancient traditions and thereby helped ensure mitigation, adaptation and other cognate concerns become home-grown in India. For more on this, see Amrita Narlikar, 'India's Role in Global Governance: A Modi-fication?' *International Affairs*, 93: 1, 2017, pp. 93–111.

6. The EU–India relationship is a classic case of this problem, see Amrita Narlikar, 'Scripting a Third Way: The Importance of EU–India Partnership,' *ORF Issue Brief No. 540*, https://www.orfonline.org/research/scripting-a-third-way/, May 2022 (originally published as part of *Raisina Files 2022*).

Chapter 4

1. Mathew Arnold, 'The Scholar-Gipsy', https://www. poetryfoundation.org/poems/43606/the-scholar-gipsy (accessed 11 August 2023).
2. In fact, the first twenty are all situated in Europe: https:// epi.yale.edu/downloads/epi2022report06062022.pdf (accessed 11 August 2023).
3. OECD Family Database, Public Spending on Family Benefits, https://www.oecd.org/els/soc/PF1_1_Public_ spending_on_family_benefits.pdf (accessed 11 August 2023).
4. OECD Family Database, 'Parental Leave Systems' https://www.oecd.org/els/soc/PF2_1_Parental_leave_ systems.pdf (accessed 11 August 2023).
5. This may seem obvious but is not always easy to find in policy documents. The German government's Strategy Paper on the Indo-Pacific is a case in point, which brings together a variety of contradictory goals (or what Boris Johnson would describe as 'cakeism'). The recently published German national security policy is also a compromise document, involving motherhood and apple pie, and weak on the necessary prioritization of goals (with resource allocation implications).

Chapter 5

1. Amrita Narlikar and Cecilia Sottilotta, 'How Not to Do Equal opportunity, Diversity and Inclusion in academia: Ten Commandments', *International Affairs Blog,* 9 December 2022, https://medium. com/international-affairs-blog/how-not-to-do-equal-opportunity-diversity-and-inclusion-in-academia-ten-

commandments-6b4bad8231c3, (accessed 11 August 2023).

2. Amrita Narlikar and Michael Zürn, work in progress.

Chapter 6

1. For a useful article that identifies the dangers and some reasons behind the shallowness of (what should be) an extremely important debate, see Haydn Washington and Helen Kopnina, 'Discussing the Silence and Denial around Population Growth and Its Environmental Impact. How Do We Find Ways Forward?' *World*, 3:4, 2022, pp. 1009–27, https://doi.org/10.3390/world3040057 (accessed 11 August 2023).
2. Elbridge Colby, "Interests, Not Values, Should Guide
3. America's China Strategy', *The National Interest*, 25 April 2021.
4. Amrita Narlikar, 'How Not To negotiate: The Case of Trade Multilateralism', *International Affairs*, 98:5, September 2022.

Chapter 7

1. For an accessible, online version of the Bhagavad Gita, see commentary by Swami Mukundananda, https://www.holy-bhagavad-gita.org/index (accessed 11 August 2023).
2. At this point in the Bhagavad Gita, it is suggested that Arjun's victory is assured; however, as Krishn reiterates through much of the text, there are no guarantees towards this. By defending righteousness and truth, Arjun is choosing the path of courage and glory. But it is uncertain whether this glory is to be

achieved through his death in battle or by his emerging as a winner to enjoy the spoils of the kingdom. The scope for human agency is thus immense, and the choice that Arjun makes—and the choices that we all make—matter.

3. For a summary of the story, refer to the Plot Line that follows the Introduction to this book.

4. Recall that one of the key lessons of the yaksh Prashn, as discussed earlier in this book, is that dharm protects those who protect it; this message fits perfectly with the non-dualism (*advaitvaad*) advanced by the Bhagavad Gita.

5. Note that this does not translate into vigilantism; rather, it involves working *roughly* with the rules of the system to defend interests and values. *Roughly* is a key word here. War, after all, does not necessarily represent change *within* the system but *of* the system; it is a deviation from rules of normality, and yet Krishn urges Arjun to take up arms, when the time comes. And even war has its rules, which should be bent only in the most extreme of circumstances (hence also the repeated appeal by Krishn to the notion of duty).

6. The BBC's documentary on India's prime minister, *The Modi Question* (2023), illustrates the latter type of misrepresentation.

7. S. Jaishankar, External Affairs Minister's Speech at the 4th Ramnath Goenka Lecture, 14 November 2019, https://www.mea.gov.in/Speeches-Statements.htm?dtl/32038 (accessed 11 August 2023).

8. S. Jaishankar, Raisina Dialogue, 2019.

Chapter 8

1. Drishtadyumn's hatred of the great teacher derived from a long-standing rivalry between King Drupad and Dronaacharya. Drupad and Dronaacharya were very close friends as students in a monastery. Drupad, however, on assuming kingship, became arrogant. He humiliated his childhood friend for his poverty and refused to help him in even meagre ways. Dronaacharya avenged this insult through the capture of Drupad's kingdom, Panchaal, with the help of his ace student, Arjun. He then returned half the kingdom to Drupad, with the goal of re-establishing economic and status parity between the two. Drupad accepted the deal but never forgot this insult. He conducted a fire sacrifice, from which emerged Drishtadyumn, with the sole purpose of avenging his father's honour. Also born from this sacrifice was Draupadi, who would wed the Pandavs. Her humiliation in the Kaurav court, whilst Dronaacharya stood silently by, only intensified Drishtadyumn's resolve to kill Dronaacharya.

2. Daniel Drezner and Amrita Narlikar (eds.), 'The How Not To Guide for International Relations', *International Affairs*, centenary special issue, 98:5, September 2022, https://academic.oup.com/ia/issue/98/5 (accessed 11 August 2023).

3. Amrita Narlikar, *Poverty Narratives and Power Paradoxes in International Trade Negotiations and Beyond* (New York: Cambridge University Press, 2020).

4. 'Joseph Goebbels: On the "Big Lie"', Jewish Virtual Library, https://www.jewishvirtuallibrary.org/joseph-

goebbels-on-the-quot-big-lie-quot (accessed 11 August 2023).

5. '"Troll Factory" Spreading Russian Pro-War Lies Online, says UK', *Guardian*, 1 May 2022, https://www.theguardian.com/world/2022/may/01/troll-factory-spreading-russian-pro-war-lies-online-says-uk (accessed 11 August 2023).

6. Amrita Narikar, 'How Not To Negotiate: The Case of Trade Multilateralism', *International Affairs,* 98:5, September 2022, pp. 1553–73, https://academic.oup.com/ia/article/98/5/1553/6686642 (accessed 11 August 2023); Rob Howse, 'From Politics to Technocracy and Back Again: The Fate of the Multilateral Trade Regime', *American Journal of International Law*, 96:1, January 2002, pp. 94–117.

7. Samir Saran and Shashank Mattoo, 'Big Tech versus Red Tech: The Diminishing of Democracy in the Digital Age', *Commentary,* Observer Research Foundation, 12 February 2022, https://www.orfonline.org/research/big-tech-vs-red-tech/ (accessed 11 August 2023).

8. Fen Osler Hampson and Paul Twomey, 'Negotiating the Internet', in Fen Osler Hampson and Amrita Narlikar (eds.), *International Negotiation and Political Narratives: A Comparative Study* (London: Routledge, 2022).

Chapter 9

1. This term is used by Matthew Leep; see 'Multispecies Security and Personhood', *Review of International Studies*, 49:2, 2023, pp. 181–200.

2. In fact, even though he is on the side of the usually villainous Kauravs, his name remains a popular one

for boys in India, even today, as is the epithet '*daanvir Karn*' (reminding us of Karn's legendary, courageous generosity).

3. On Karn's pride and his inferiority complex, see V.S. Sukthankar, *On the Meaning of the Mahabharata* (Bombay: The Asiatic Society of Bombay, 1957), Monograph IV.

4. For a classic on Krishn, see Bimal Krishna Matilal, 'Krsna: In Defence of a Devious Deity', in Jonardon Ganeri (ed.), *Ethics and Epics: The Collected Essays of Bimal Krishna Matilal,* Vol. 2 (Oxford: Oxford University Press, 2002).

5. Jaishankar, Raisina Dialogue, 2019.

6. Ents are the shepherds of the forests in the fantasy world of Middle-Earth created by J.R.R. Tolkein and exhibit similar caution in taking sides. This analogy was first drawn in Amrita Narlikar, 'Scripting a Third Way: The Importance of EU–India Partnership', *Raisina Files 2022*; republished as *ORF Issue Brief*, no. 540, May 2022, https://www.orfonline.org/research/scripting-a-third-way/(accessed 11 August 2023); for details of the argument presented here, please refer to the same.

7. As recommended by India's foreign minister, e.g. External Affairs Minister's Speech at the 4th Ramnath Goenka Lecture, 14 November 2019, https://www.mea.gov.in/Speeches-Statements.htm?dtl/32038 (accessed 11 August 2023).

8. For other examples, see Daniel Drezner and Amrita Narlikar, 'The How Not To Guide for International Relations', guest-edited centenary special issue, *International Affairs,* 98:5, 2022, https://academic.oup.com/ia/article/98/5/1499/6686625 (accessed 11 August 2023).

9. Amrita Narlikar, 'How Not To Negotiate: The Case of Trade Multilateralism', *International Affairs,* 98:5, 2022, pp. 1553–73, https://academic.oup.com/ia/article/98/5/1553/6686642; Amitabh Mattoo, 'How Not To Deal With A Rising China: A Perspective From South Asia', *International Affairs,* 98:5, 2022, pp. 1653–75, https://academic.oup.com/ia/article/98/5/1653/6686609 (accessed 11 August 2023).

10. Several chapters in this book show how these apparent contradictions can be reconciled, including the chapter on the yaksh Prashn.

Chapter 10

1. For example, Kevin Jon Heller, 'Norway Murders Freya the Walrus', Opinio Juris, 15 August 2022, http://opiniojuris.org/2022/08/15/norway-murders-freya-the-walrus/ (accessed 11 August 2023).

2. Valeria Roman, 'Argentina Grants an Orangutan Human-Like Rights', *Scientific American*, 9 January 2015, https://www.scientificamerican.com/article/argentina-grants-an-orangutan-human-like-rights/ (accessed 11 August 2023).

3. Greta Thunberg, *UN Climate Action Summit,* 23 September 2019, https://www.un.org/development/desa/youth/news/2019/09/greta-thunberg/ (accessed 11 August 2023).

4. Green parties across Europe should be the ones closest to the cause of environmentalism and ecologism.

5. Amrita Narlikar, 'German Feminist Foreign Policy: An Inside–Outside Perspective', *Raisina Debates,*

Observer Research Foundation, 12 September 2022, https://www.orfonline.org/expert-speak/german-feminist-foreign-policy/ (accessed 11 August 2023).

6. For example, Raimundo Panikkar, 'Is the Notion of Human Rights a western concept?', *Diogenes*, 30:120, 1982, pp. 75–102.

7. More on this in the following chapter.

8. Amrita Narlikar and Cecilia Sottilotta, 'Pandemic Narratives and Policy Responses: West European governments and COVID19', *Journal of European Public Policy*, 28:8, 2021, pp. 1238–57, first published online on 19 June 2021, https://www.tandfonline.com/doi/abs/10.1080/13501763.2021.1942152?journalCode=rjpp20 (accessed 11 August 2023).

9. Jeanine Santucci, 'A Letter to My Loved Ones about COVID-19: You've Moved On, but I'm Still Here', *USA Today*, 19 March 2023, https://eu.usatoday.com/story/opinion/voices/2023/03/19/covid-pandemic-not-over-high-risk/11472097002/ (accessed 11 August 2023).

10. For example, https://twitter.com/drclairetaylor/status/1642374808821284867 (accessed 11 August 2023); https://twitter.com/EricTopol/status/1613965639609372673 (accessed 11 August 2023); https://twitter.com/DrEricDing/status/1639640365660532736 (accessed 11 August 2023).

11. Lord Palmerston, Speech, House of Commons, 1 March 1848, https://api.parliament.uk/historic-hansard/commons/1848/mar/01/treaty-of-adrianople-charges-against (accessed 11 August 2023).

Chapter 11

1. For a recitation of this verse and its application to debates on climate change, see https://www.youtube. com/watch?v=PkwJn7m4je4 (accessed 11 August 2023).

2. We are seeing elements of this being brought to life via the G20 process under India's presidency, whose chosen motto of 'One earth, one family, one future' is inspired from this idea. T20 TaskForce 3 on LiFE (Resiliences, Values and Well-being), of which one of the authors of this book is a co-chair, is novel in the T20 process to flag up these issues. How far India will be able to go in de-anthropocizing national and global debates remains to be seen, though. Amrita Narlikar lays out an agenda towards this and also points to some of the challenges: 'Ancient Wisdom for Today and Tomorrow: India's Presidency of the G20', in Samir Saran and Vinia Mukherjee (eds.), *Adrift at Sea: Lighthouse in the Tempest?*, *Raisina Files,* Volume 7, March 2023, pp. 116–122, https://www.orfonline.org/ wp-content/uploads/2023/02/ORF_RaisinaFiles2023. pdf (accessed 11 August 2023).

3. David Benatar, 'Our Cruel Treatment of Animals led to the Coronavirus', *New York Times,* 13 April 2020. On zoonotic spillover, see for instance, Alyssa Marchese and Alice Hovorka, 'Zoonoses Transfer, Factory Farms and Unsustainable Human–Animal Relations', *Sustainability,* 14:19, 12806, October 2022.

4. https://education.nationalgeographic.org/resource/ conservation/(accessed 11 August 2023).

5. For example, Markus Frauendorfer, 'The Rediscovery of Indigenous Thought in the Modern Legal System: The Case of the Great Apes', *Global Policy,* 9:1, February 2018, pp. 17–25.

6. For an excellent overview of these debates, see Matthew Leep, 'Multispecies Security and Personhood', *Review of International Studies,* 49:2, 2023, pp. 181–200.

7. In the Indian case, this would mean an amendment and updating of the Prevention of Cruelty to Animals Act (1960). For instance, Chapter III, Article 11, of the PCA, states the penalty and punishment for cruelty to animals as:

> . . . in the case of a first offence, with fine which shall not be less than ten rupees but which may extend to fifty rupees and in the case of a second or subsequent offence committed within three years of the previous offence, with fine which shall not be less than twenty-five rupees but which may extend to one hundred rupees or with imprisonment for a term which may extend to three months, or with both. (PCA, 1960 https://www.indiacode.nic.in/bitstream/123456789/11237/1/the_prevention_of_cruelty_to_animals_act%2C_1960.pdf).

> Such low penalties seem to no longer serve as a deterrent against abuse of animals; perhaps they even send a perverse signal on how undervalued animals are in Indian society.

Scan QR code to access the
Penguin Random House India website